VANTAGE

Full-spectrum thinking grew
out of Institute for the Future's
foundational forecasts, and
provides a lens for breaking apart
traditional silos of thought and
action, a critical skill for building
your future-ready organization.

www.iftf.org/vantage

Praise for *Full-Spectrum Thinking*

"This is a great read that energizes me. Leaders must engage with humility and courage to set clear direction—but look to their teams for the best execution across a spectrum of possibilities. Right or wrong is a fallacy that must be replaced by opportunities to dynamically decide, test, and adapt."
—Jason Field, President and CEO, W. L. Gore & Associates

"*Full-Spectrum Thinking* challenges us to be courageous as we knit together what humans do best with the power of computing for better outcomes at greater speed. We need to inspire human resources leaders to be the role models of try, fail fast and cheap—and try again as we build tools, frameworks, and experiences that enable our companies and teams to excel in the digital world."
—Vicki Lostetter, Chief Human Resources Officer, WestRock

"*Full-Spectrum Thinking* is just the right book at just the right time, giving us new tools, new ways of sense-making, and new hope. This will be the book I hand out to everyone who works with me, as well as to friends and family."
—Paul LeBlanc, President, Southern New Hampshire University

"Design thinking will blend with futures thinking in the near future. The mindset of *Full-Spectrum Thinking* will be needed to leap beyond the narrow categories of thought that constrain much of today's innovation."
—Tim Brown, Chair, IDEO

"Bob Johansen and the Institute for the Future have helped United Rentals enhance our spectrum of products, services, and insights for jobs that require equipment and expertise you may not want to own or have in house. New spectrums of business value will be needed to create profitable businesses in the future."
—Matt Flannery, CEO, United Rentals

"Bob Johansen has once again defined what it means to be an 'original contributor.' The insights and suggested responses contained in *Full-Spectrum Thinking* define a unique way to analyze and respond to our rapidly changing world. I will recommend this book to every board member and executive in my network."
—James I. Cash, founder of The Cash Catalyst, LLC, and Professor Emeritus, Harvard Business School

"You must read this book. It comes from a mind trained to live ten years in the future and a heart eager to get us there safely."
—Commissioner Kenneth G. Hodder, Territorial Commander, The Salvation Army

"The future has no map, especially in this era of rapid change. Agile open-mindedness is essential to navigate it, and Bob Johansen's *Full-Spectrum Thinking* lays out a clear path for how to get there. For starters, reject rigid categories that 'coerce,' 'keep us in cages,' and 'move us away from understanding the bigger

picture.' Seek clarity and context because the emerging future will be one with fluid roles and identities. Leaders will need to be 'very clear about where they want to go but very flexible about how they get there.' This insightful book is for all those interested in enhancing their own agility in how they think about and face the future."
   —Mary Kay Magistad, creator and host of the *Whose Century Is It?* podcast and former China correspondent, NPR and PRI/BBC's *The World*

"Classic departmental-based organizational thinking is the most prolific barrier to enterprise value maximization. *Full-Spectrum Thinking* empowers our holistic view of the consumer that is fundamental to personalized guest experience creation."
   —John Padgett, Chief Innovation Officer, Carnival Corporation

"In his books, his workshops, and the countless friendships like ours that he's built over the past thirty years, Bob has helped a generation of leaders better anticipate future challenges and opportunities. He's done it again with *Full-Spectrum Thinking*, which provides the framework to evaluate new opportunities, experiences, and people through a broader lens. Leaders concerned about future-proofing their organizations should read this book."
   —Scott Price, Chief Strategy and Transformation Officer, UPS

"Bob Johansen continues to demonstrate thought leadership in preparing for a more positive future. His new *Full-Spectrum Thinking* extends our Army War College Strategic Thinking Framework. In doing so, it requires our leaders to resist the certainty lure of heuristics, actively challenge categorizing assumptions, and seek greater inclusiveness in generating better possibilities for the future."
   —Charles D. Allen, Professor of Leadership and Cultural Studies, US Army War College

"A future-back mindset and full-spectrum thinking are needed urgently to create a vision and strategy that is not stuck in the tired categories of the past."
   —Mark W. Johnson, cofounder of Innosight

"The process of naming nature, or communicating it through language at all, involves fragmenting what is essentially an undivided evolutionary continuum. *Full-Spectrum Thinking* is a critical plea for humans to think more fluidly, beyond the boxes and labels, to overcome the urge to reduce, simplify, and fragment nature."
   —James Prosek, artist, writer, and naturalist

"Bob Johansen is proposing a fundamental shift in how we form our shared stories of identity, organizations, and world vision. He is applying the science of the story to the art of communication."
   —Kendall Haven, story consultant, author, and master storyteller

"The wisdom of *Full-Spectrum Thinking* is enduring, but the new tools will make it scalable globally."
   —Robert A. McDonald, Eighth Secretary, Department of Veterans Affairs, and retired Chairman, President, and CEO, Procter & Gamble

FULL-SPECTRUM
THINKING

Also authored or coauthored by Bob Johansen

Electronic Meetings

Teleconferencing and Beyond

Leading Business Teams

Groupware

GlobalWork

Upsizing the Individual in the Downsized Organization

Get There Early

Leaders Make the Future

The Reciprocity Advantage

The New Leadership Literacies

FULL-SPECTRUM THINKING

How to
Escape Boxes in a
Post-Categorical Future

BOB JOHANSEN
INSTITUTE FOR THE FUTURE

Berrett–Koehler Publishers, Inc.

All royalties from this book go to

INSTITUTE FOR THE FUTURE'S

nonprofit leadership development programs.

Berrett-Koehler Publishers, Inc.
1333 Broadway, Suite 1000
Oakland, CA 94612-1921
Tel: (510) 817-2277 / Fax: (510) 817-2278
www.bkconnection.com

ORDERING INFORMATION

QUANTITY SALES.
Special discounts are available on quantity purchases by corporations, associations, and others. For details, contact the "Special Sales Department" at the Berrett-Koehler address above.
INDIVIDUAL SALES.
Berrett-Koehler publications are available through most bookstores. They can also be ordered directly from Berrett-Koehler: Tel: (800) 929-2929; Fax: (802) 864-7626; www.bkconnection.com.
ORDERS FOR COLLEGE TEXTBOOK/COURSE ADOPTION USE.
Please contact Berrett-Koehler: Tel: (800) 929-2929; Fax: (802) 864-7626.

Distributed to the US trade and internationally by Penguin Random House Publisher Services.

Berrett-Koehler and the BK logo are registered trademarks of Berrett-Koehler Publishers, Inc.

Printed in Canada

Berrett-Koehler books are printed on long-lasting acid-free paper. When it is available, we choose paper that has been manufactured by environmentally responsible processes. These may include using trees grown in sustainable forests, incorporating recycled paper, minimizing chlorine in bleaching, or recycling the energy produced at the paper mill.

Library of Congress Cataloging-in-Publication Data
Names: Johansen, Robert, author.
Title: Full-spectrum thinking : how to escape boxes in a post-categorical future / Bob Johansen.
Description: First edition. | Oakland, CA : Berrett-Koehler Publishers, [2020] | Includes bibliographical references and index.
Identifiers: LCCN 2019054215 | ISBN 9781523087518 (hardcover) | ISBN 9781523087525 (pdf) | ISBN 9781523087532 (epub)
Subjects: LCSH: Leadership. | Executive ability.
Classification: LCC HD57.7 .J633 2021 | DDC 658.4/092—dc23
LC record available at https://lccn.loc.gov/2019054215

FIRST EDITION

28 27 26 25 24 23 22 21 20 || 10 9 8 7 6 5 4 3 2 1

Book producer: BookMatters | Text designer: BookMatters | Jacket designer: Archie Ferguson | Jacket illustrator: Andy Gilmore | Copyeditor: Lou Doucette | Proofer: Janet Reed Blake | Indexer: Leonard Rosenbaum

To Robin,
Cory and Amanda, Lisa and Zach,
Nico and Everett, Robbie and Nate,
and Atticus

Full-spectrum thinking
is the ability to seek patterns and clarity
across gradients of possibility—
outside, across, beyond, or maybe even without
any boxes or categories—while
resisting false certainty.

CONTENTS

Please look inside the book jacket
for a visual summary of the book.

The Core Story

WHAT CATEGORIES DO YOU USE TO DESCRIBE YOURSELF?

I like to ask this question at the beginning of workshops, and I'm always surprised by how many different categories people use to describe themselves: mother, father, manager, accountant, leader, board member, soldier, cook, gardener, writer, and so on. Quickly listing 20 categories to describe oneself is not uncommon.

How many different categories does it take before you start thinking of yourself across a broad spectrum?

Categories coerce. Categories are thrown at people like capture nets over wild animals. Categories keep us in cages. Categories can kill.

Full-spectrum[1] thinking is the ability to seek patterns and clarity across gradients of possibility—outside, across, beyond, or maybe even without any boxes or categories—while resisting false certainty.

In today's political climate, categories dumb down the way we talk about each other. Categorical thinking moves us away from understanding the bigger picture. It lacks context. Categories lead us toward certainty, but away from clarity.

Full-spectrum thinking has the potential to diffuse polarities, to reveal that our differences are not as stark as they seem through the narrow lens of categories. My colleague Toshi Hoo, who leads Institute for the Future's Emerging Media Lab, commented to me that full-spectrum thinking helps us find the multidimensional ways in which things are connected—not just the ways in which they are distinct from each other.

Think of the best leaders you have ever had, the people who inspired you the most.

How did those leaders categorize themselves?

How did they categorize you and others?

My guess is that your best leaders didn't categorize others mindlessly. They made you feel recognized and empowered—but not stereotyped. They used appropriate categories to define your strengths and highlight your contributions, rather than pigeonhole you or degrade your efforts. They didn't box you in or categorize you as something you are not. They saw the full amplitude of your potential. My guess is that your best leaders were clear about the future but rarely spoke in certainties.

This book is about how to seed and nurture a mindset that expands the characteristics that you already admire in the best leaders. Full-spectrum thinking fosters empathy. Mindless categorizing fosters contempt. Categories make it easy to write off others with tired labels like "immigrant," "black," "white," "millennial," "gay," "Jew," "Muslim," or "old." Choosing an identity for yourself is one thing, but being labeled by others is quite another—and the way you say it can be just as important as what you say.

The way forward is to develop full-spectrum thinking—not by advocating for our own stereotypes of others or by creating new boxes to throw people into without careful thought.

Being stuck in categorical thought doesn't actually involve much thinking at all—you just assume without thinking that new experiences will fit into your old boxes, buckets, labels, generalizations, and stereotypes. Knee-jerk categorization of others is reckless. Even if after careful thought you decide to categorize, you should start by thinking about a full spectrum of possibilities first.

Categorizing is a convenient and time-honored strategy for gaining and maintaining power. Categorization can have psychological or material benefits by helping you develop your own identity and community. But lazy or careless categorizing of others is dangerous—and it will get even more dangerous in the future. Fortunately, a gradual shift from categorical to full-spectrum thinking has already begun.

Elite basketball players, for example, used to be categorized as a 1 (point guard), a 2 (shooting guard), a 3 (small forward), a 4 (power forward), or a 5 (center). Then came Magic Johnson and later LeBron James, and now even more broad-spectrum players can play more than one position. Categorizing basketball players no longer works in the same way it did. Today's best players are position fluid. They cannot be categorized easily or consistently. The serious players all have a spectrum of talents that defy static categories. They play multiposition—I'd call it full-spectrum—basketball.

But it won't be a total flip from categorical to full-spectrum thinking. I'm not against categories if they are accurate and fair and do no harm. All of us need to create structures and categories of some kind that work for us and for others. The categories that we choose can be empowering.

The best scientists, for example, learn how to use categories without being deluded by them. Categories have a long history and at times have been very useful. Nevertheless, John Fowles argued that we have become so steeped in categorical thinking that we sometimes cannot experience the spectrum of possibilities that the world around us offers. Often, we cannot see the forest because we're so focused on naming the trees.[2]

Full-spectrum thinking will apply across all levels of aggregation: individual, organizational, and societal. In the future, full-spectrum thinking will become both more necessary and less difficult because of a new range of tools.

A fresh mix of new and old technology and media tools will enable—and then require—full-spectrum thinking. Over the next decade, the current tools for full-spectrum thinking will get dramatically better, just as the need for more nuanced ways of perceiving and judging the outside world will increase.

Powerful digital media—including gameful engagement, big data analytics, visualization, blockchain, and machine learning—will be both more powerful and easier to use. New clarity filters will get practical just as the need becomes urgent. Digitally amplified full-spectrum thinking will help us resist the temptations of premature categorization and false certainty. It will be an antidote to the dangerous polarization of today.

Full-spectrum thinking has the potential to reveal that commonalities are hidden in plain view. Full-spectrum thinking is about recognizing patterns, seeking clarity, and resisting certainty. A full-spectrum mindset is a great place to start in order to make sense out of ourselves, the world around us, and the future. It provides context. It encourages nuance.

Even though unexamined categorical thinking remains in force and is unconsciously followed in many fields, a more positive future is coming that will allow us to be much more nuanced and hopeful. The preferable future will be an intelligent blend of cautious categorical and disciplined full-spectrum thinking.

Increasingly, we will be able to use new digital tools for full-spectrum thinking to achieve breakthroughs in business, leadership, innovation, politics, community relations, and many other domains. Sloppy categorical thinking, so common today, will be inexcusable and embarrassing in the future.

The future will be a scramble: an asymmetrical patchwork of urgency, panic, imbalance, and hope. Full-spectrum thinking will make people more future-ready and better able to make sense out of new opportunities and threats. Some people practice full-spectrum thinking already, and their efforts will become more visible and powerful. It will also be much easier for novices to develop their own full-spectrum thinking abilities.

We will move toward—but never quite reach—a post-categorical future that will reward rigorous full-spectrum thinking. Categories won't disappear, but they will be far less coercive.

This book is about why now is the time to shift from categorical toward full-spectrum thinking. It will help you become more of a full-spectrum thinker. It will guide you in creating organizations that value and benefit from full-spectrum thinking. I have three goals in this book:

1. Improve how people think about the past, the present, and the future.

2. Improve how organizations identify and evaluate new business opportunities.

3. Depolarize strategic conversations to allow for a wider range of alternatives beyond binary choices.

This book is designed for use in training and executive development programs for corporations, nonprofits, government agencies, and the military. It is written for hiring managers, chief talent officers, CHROs, CEOs, CIOs, and innovators of all kinds.

The Conclusion includes a series of guidelines, tools, and actions you can take now to develop your own full-spectrum thinking mindset as well as spread this kind of thinking across your organization.

I want this book to seed and nurture full-spectrum thinking and a next generation of full-spectrum thinkers. My purpose is to encourage business leaders, educators, public officials, and individual people to think beyond simplistic labels, categories, boxes, slots, or buckets. The dangers of certitude are swelling.

Full-Spectrum Thinking can be read on its own or in concert with *The New Leadership Literacies* and *Leaders Make the Future*. In *Full-Spectrum Thinking*, I focus on the *mindset* that will be required to win in the future—and make the world a better place. I began this trilogy after my experiences at the Army War College, when I asked what kind of *skills* would be necessary for leaders to thrive in the post-9/11 world. Then, I became intrigued with leadership *literacies*—the disciplines and practices of leadership—beyond skills. I recommend that you begin with mindset, then consider literacies and skills.

This book flows through three related parts:

- Part One is focused on the core concepts and how futures thinking and full-spectrum thinking can break us out of the categorical constraints of the past and present.

- Part Two is focused on the emerging tools, the networks, and the true digital natives who will engage with the scrambled world around us and expand full-spectrum thinking on a global scale.

- Part Three is focused on the future that is already beginning today.

It will show you examples of broader spectrums and new applications that will become possible first, then mandatory.

New spectrums of meaning will become possible as people see the future with more clarity, but less certainty.

Many people are certain, but few are clear.

That's about to change.

PART ONE

THE PAST CANNOT CONTINUE

THE FUTURE WILL PUNISH CATEGORICAL THINKING BUT reward full-spectrum thinking.

The future will be a global *scramble* that will be very difficult to categorize. You will need a full-spectrum mindset to have any hint of what is going on. The next decade will see staggering shifts like the increasingly visible rich-poor and asset gap, cyber warfare and cybercrime, and global climate disruption.

The scramble will be fraught with toxic misinformation (not necessarily intentional), disinformation (intentional), and distrust. In this future, it will be very dangerous to force fit new threats or new opportunities into old categories of thought. Fortunately, new spectrums of thought will become possible in new ways over the next decade. Full-spectrum thinking will be required in order to thrive.

If you have a carton of eggs, as the old folk story goes, you can decide how you want to cook them. Once you've scrambled the eggs, you cannot unscramble them. You can, however, make the scrambled eggs into some kind of new egg-based dish.

During the scramble, many things that have been stuck will become unstuck. Some things will unravel. The scramblers of the present world—we see them all around us today—won't be very good at putting things back together again.

In the scrambled future I am forecasting, you can expect an unusual number of unexpected consequences from the scrambling. You will have a range of creative new options that weren't on the menu in the past. The future will get even more perplexing over the next decade, and most people—including most leaders—are not ready.

Our old categories will work adequately when new opportunities or threats match prior understanding. Simplistic categorization, however, will be perilous if people stereotype others superficially or boil new experiences down too far or too fast. People categorize to try to understand, but categorization often yields a superficial or false understanding. Sometimes categorizing demeans or devalues others.

A full-spectrum mindset is not new. In fact, full-spectrum thinking was probably more common among our ancestors than it is now. You can argue that children are born with it until we crush it out of them with labels, rigid intelligence and educational testing, autofill tools, and binary computing where everything ultimately must be reduced to a zero or a one.

In the effort to create simple stories to help people understand the scramble, *overly simplistic* stories will abound—especially those created by extreme politicians and extreme religions. People will struggle to make sense of emerging futures that often won't make much sense at all. Comforting labels will be both alluring and fraught with danger.

Full-spectrum thinking is, in a way, a step back to analog even as it is a step forward to an ever more digitally enhanced world.

Producer George Martin joined the Beatles just as they tired of live performances because of the inane screaming of fans. He was a practitioner of full-spectrum thinking before it was called that. His mentality was to move beyond the live performance to something different that was a kind of hybrid of analog and digital. He didn't try to simulate concert performances; he tried to create something profoundly different and, at least in some ways, better. He was thinking beyond either/or. Now, analog has shifted to digital in the music world, but at a price that sometimes comes at a cost of reduced quality to the ears of those who prefer vinyl records.

Now, we can—as George Martin and the later Beatles did for music—create a new spectrum of experiences that has the nuances of the analog world with the power and scale of digital.

Thinking across spectrums (not even just one spectrum) will become much easier. Our brains are very good at putting new things into old boxes. Next-generation tools and networks will help us teach our brains the new tricks of full-spectrum thinking.

Neuroscience (an important influence for this book) teaches us that our brains are very good at putting new experiences in old categories. Simplistic categorization will be perilous, however.

Neuroscientist Kevin Ochsner, a Columbia professor, was the respondent to my keynote speech at the NeuroLeadership Summit on October 4, 2018, in New York. I talked about the value of strategic foresight and futures thinking. Professor Ochsner's response was that foresight can "lift us up from the eternal present," where our brains function by default.

Our brains, he went on, have evolved to constantly categorize and predict what's next—to try to keep us safe and out of trouble. Even though predicting the future is impossible, our brains do it anyway. When faced with a confusing situation, our brains' default reaction is fear and dread, fight or flight. Our brains were programmed in the past to do continuous prediction of what's coming next. The brain practices of the past, however, will get us into a lot of trouble in the future.

The emerging future will require us to teach our brains new tricks, to move from unexamined categorical thinking to mindful full-spectrum thinking. Sometimes categories are weaponized to inflict violence. Sometimes people categorize to pretend they understand. Sometimes people categorize to demean or devalue others.

Full-spectrum thinking will help people strategize with a future-back approach (I call it Now, FUTURE, Next), which we have an urgent need to do in order to thrive in the scramble. This book shows you how to do that.

Many people today—including some of the most popular political and religious leaders—think only within their own rigid boxes of thought. Some leaders, however, have developed an ability to think across the boxes, and those are the ones who deserve our attention.

This part of the book will show why we cannot continue to be locked in categorical thinking. Chapter 1 introduces full-spectrum thinking at the individual, organizational, and societal levels. Chapter 2 explores the dilemma of categories that were intended to help us understand what is around us but which we often take too seriously. Then, Chapter 3 introduces futures thinking to help us move beyond the past and make a better future.

Chapter 1

Ramping Up to Full-Spectrum Thinking

More Clarity, Less Certainty

Chapter 2

The Coercion of Categories

Please Don't Stamp Me with **Your** *Label*

Chapter 3

Escape the Boxes of the Past

How to Use Futures Thinking

Categorical thinking allows little room for subtle differences. Full-spectrum thinking is both nuanced and scalable. Tension will remain, since cultures are very good at detecting and reinforcing categories, but the spectrum of possibilities will continue to broaden.

For example, people talk about being online or offline—but that will be increasingly difficult as our connectivity grows. Ten years from now, there will be a spectrum of online/offline realities. Today, most of us are offline unless we are on. In the future, most of us will be online unless we are off. It will seem quaintly out of touch to distinguish between being online and offline. "Logging onto the internet" will be a foreign concept with no meaning except to very old or out-of-touch people.

Categories won't go away, and simple categories will work fine when they accurately match a new situation to an old one. But simplistic categories, labels, generalizations, and stereotypes will be exposed for what they are: sloppy and dangerous. Racism, sexism, and other prejudices will be much harder to justify in a world of everyday full-spectrum thinking skills and capabilities.

Priority Questions for Part One

As an individual, how can you constructively question your unexamined assumptions about categorizing yourself and others?

As an organization, how can you categorize mindfully and in ways that draw out the best in people rather than boxing them in? How can you consider a broader range of business and social value that you might deliver?

How can societies avoid the dangers of stereotyping? How can societies and cultures seed and employ full-spectrum thinking in order to make the future a better place and space?

CHAPTER 1

Ramping Up to Full-Spectrum Thinking

More Clarity, Less Certainty

SOFT DRINK CANS, HALF OF THEM STILL BOUND TOGETHER with plastic collars, were scattered across a coffee table in the small family room when we arrived in the early afternoon to visit Peter Drucker in his 95th year, about a year before he died in 2005. We were there to talk with the famous management guru[1] about the future of work and the human resources function.

I walked into that room with AG Lafley, then the CEO of Procter & Gamble; Dick Antoine, P&G's head of human resources; and Craig Wynett, a visionary P&G thinker. I felt fortunate to have been invited and was impressed by the fact that the CEO of one of the world's best companies had flown across the country in his corporate jet to spend the afternoon with this remarkable 94-year-old.

We were told in advance that we would be meeting in a simple setting with no staff support, but Peter Drucker welcomed us warmly to his modest ranch-style house in Claremont, California—just a short walk from the Drucker School of Management at Claremont Graduate University. Peter Drucker was slow in body by that time in his life, but still very active in mind. My brief time with him was mindset altering and has become the anchor story for this book.

He told us that for the first half of your life, you should try many different kinds of work and make it a point to work with many different kinds of people—since you won't yet know who you are or what you want to become. Try out a spectrum of possibilities, he taught us.

For the second half of life, Drucker said, you should only work on things you are passionate about and only work with people with whom you love to work. Focus is good, he said, but don't focus too early. Categories of work aren't necessarily bad, unless they lock you into a categorical cage.

By "first half of life," since he was approaching 100 years of age at the time and still thinking strong, I took him to mean about 50 years. Now, more than 20 years later, I realize that Peter Drucker was encouraging us to have a full-spectrum mindset about work and life—especially at key milestones. I realize now that he was thinking across all levels of aggregation: individual, organizational, and societal.

Look beyond Binary Choices

Peter Drucker was encouraging us to see beyond the caging and coercion of categories. Try many kinds of work while you are less than 50 years old. Don't allow people (like your parents or your friends or your professors or your first boss or your company) to categorize you too soon or label you as this or that. Don't box yourself into a job or a career trajectory that is not a calling for you. Search for a vocation, not just a job.

Many parents I know just assume that their kids will go to college. Many of their kids, however, aren't so sure. Many young people are not sure what they want to do, they are not sure about the value of a college degree, and they don't want student loan debt. Stalemated by the binary choice of college or not, a growing number of families are choosing a gap year when a young person can explore. The gap year is a simple example of broader-spectrum thinking.

Parents often have more specific expectations than their kids. My young colleague Gabe Cervantes became my research assistant after graduating from Williams College as a first-generation college student and first-generation American-born (his parents immigrated from Mexico). When he joined me, he had already done a few different things since graduating and was on his way to law school when he decided instead to join Institute for the Future (IFTF) and work on this book with me. His family was shocked: they wanted a lawyer for a son—not a futurist. In fact, they had never heard of a career category called futurist. Gabe had a goal that he had shared with his parents: go to law school and work his way up to the point where he could advise senior executives at corporations. He chose working with me so that he could have the experience of working with top executives sooner, but this was not a path that his parents understood or could even imagine. Gabe may still go to law school, but he wanted a wider experience before making that choice.

Peter Drucker urged those P&G executives to offer their workers many options and assist them in navigating obstacles and choices. Don't assume that people will follow those career tracks routinely. Encourage people to go off the rails now and again.

Most people do not find a calling early in life. Many people never do find a calling. Many people work for long hours and many years in jobs they don't even like, let alone love. Drucker himself began as a journalist and had at least six distinct careers in his life. He had definitely found his calling long before we met him that sunny afternoon, but it wasn't until his mid-60s that he settled down and focused on his true calling.

Just after AG Lafley first became CEO of Procter & Gamble, his first official speech was in Chicago for the P&G alumni network. Up to that point, P&G—a bastion of employment from within—hadn't even acknowledged the existence of the P&G alumni network. The alumni were often viewed as an annoyance. In that speech, Lafley embraced the alumni as part of the global family of P&G and a powerful network that included both full-time employees and alumni. This message was very well received.

The common wisdom outside P&G was that working even a few years at the company was a terrific resume builder—perhaps equivalent to an MBA. The common wisdom within the company was that employees had to move up or out. P&G promoted from within and rarely recruited senior leaders from the outside. I have worked on projects with P&G since just after I got out of graduate school, but I learned early on in my work with them that when someone left the company, I wasn't supposed to talk about them anymore. When they left P&G, it seemed to me, it was as if they had died, or at least their lives were somehow diminished because they left the mother ship. AG Lafley changed that feeling.

AG Lafley was very attracted to Drucker's notion of experimenting widely in life. He told me, when I showed him a draft of this chapter, that he had changed majors every year in college: math to English to French to history. He once invested 47 weeks just to become fluent in Hebrew. He loaded freight cars for the railroad, ran punch presses and riveting machines in a metal fabrication factory, and taught several different courses as a substitute teacher in high school. He didn't start at P&G until he was 30. In an e-mail to me, AG Lafley reflected back on our afternoon with Peter Drucker: "I believe Drucker was right about not settling, not getting trapped in a category or a career."

Employment vs. Employability

When he became CEO, Lafley observed that P&G could no longer promise lifelong employment but that the company could and would offer lifelong *employability*. This was a major shift toward full-spectrum thinking about work and life.

The P&G diaspora of former employees (the "lost children," as longtime employees sometimes called them with a wink) was finally recognized by the new CEO. P&G is still largely a promote-from-within company, but it is a more inclusive network now. There is a full spectrum of possibilities for how you can work and how you can stay engaged with the P&G community, whether or not you are a full-time employee. Even though I have never been a P&G employee, I feel very much a part of the P&G diaspora.

This giant company has gradually shifted from thinking of P&G employees as either in or out. It is no longer a binary choice. Once people become part of the P&G diaspora in any way, they are in for life.

It seemed like bad news at the time for workers who had hoped for a job for life, but it turns out that—in the long run—it was good news. Being employable for multiple opportunities in life is much better than being locked into a job you don't like for life. There is now a full spectrum of ways to work with P&G, including the possibility—not a promise—of a full-time job for life. Being associated with P&G is a good thing.

I've learned a similar lesson with employees at Institute for the Future. I invest a lot in the young people we bring into the Institute, and I used to find it very painful when they decided to leave. Now, I've learned that leaving IFTF doesn't mean the end, it means the beginning of a new kind of relationship. Sometimes, former full-time employees become clients, and other times they become new kinds of colleagues. I had a limited view of what it meant to be an employee.

Categories limit our vision. Categories coerce. Categories can be cages.

What categories should you be using to describe yourself? What categories do you use to describe others? Over the next decade we will move gradually from rigid categorical to flexible full-spectrum thinking for individuals (yourself and others), organizations of all kinds (including businesses, nonprofits, religious organizations, and governments), and societies. Here are some examples of the broader-spectrum shift that is coming as we ramp up to full-spectrum thinking.

Full-Spectrum Thinking for Individuals

As shown in Table 1.1, each individual is shifting toward multiple identities that will become increasingly important as the next generation of the internet scales globally and virtual identities become as important as in-person identities. Each person will in fact be many different identities at different times and different places.

Adopting an identity for yourself can be an important way to develop community with others. Categorizing is one way to develop an identity and sense of self-worth. For some people, it is also important to categorize who you are *not*. For many people, their sense of self is defined by a category: I'm Black or I'm a Christian or I'm a Jew or I'm queer or I'm a professor. Identities, however, will become more fluid and multilayered.

TABLE 1.1 Full-Spectrum Thinking for Individuals

From Categorical	Toward Full Spectrum
Each person is categorized with a single role or title.	Each person will have multiple roles, with fewer titles.
Each person has a fixed identity.	Each person will have multiple, fluid, and multilayered identities in physical and virtual space.
Shoppers are considered passive consumers of products.	Expect active and engaged shoppers in search of products, services, experiences, and personal transformations.

Categorizing others is much more problematic and risky. It can be judgmental and demeaning. Gradually, people and institutions are becoming more aware of how they categorize others.

In the past, advertising was often based on segmentation, breaking consumers down into target markets. The consumer of the future, however, will be much harder to categorize. Each person will be multiple identities in mixed virtual and in-person worlds. The consumer of the future won't even like being called a "consumer," because that term will be way too passive. Each person will be an identity of multiples. Fortunately, new digital tools will help us think across a continuum of possibilities—not just force people into categories.

Instead of labeling the people who buy their products as "consumers," companies will call them "people" and will seek to understand the different identities that people adopt actively at different times in their lives. At Walt Disney World and Target, for example, consumers are called "guests."

Full-Spectrum Thinking for Organizations

How do today's organizations categorize? How will this range of possibilities change in the future? What types of organization attract you the most?

As Table 1.2 shows, organizational forms will become increasingly fluid.

TABLE 1.2 Full-Spectrum Thinking for Organizations

From Categorical	Toward Full Spectrum
Traditional jobs	More gigs and other less formal and more flexible ways of making a living without having a job
Single specialized roles like manager, staff, leader, follower, employee	Many hybrid roles for each person, with fewer full-time jobs, more computer augmentation, and some job automation
Command-and-control	Leaders who are very clear about where they want to go, but very flexible about how you will get there
Fixed hierarchies with rigid organization charts and reporting lines	More shape-shifting organizations where hierarchies come and go
Centralized authority	Distributed authority
Focus on products	Focus on a spectrum of business value from products to services to subscriptions to experiences to transformations
More closed and inward facing	More open and outward facing

Rigid hierarchies will still work in slow-moving predictable environments, but that kind of stability will be rare. For most of us, we are in a continuing rotation of being leaders and followers.

Command-and-control hierarchies just don't work as well in fast-changing unpredictable environments. In Chapter 8, I will discuss how the military has developed more flexible forms of hierarchy that still have clear commander's intent, but much more flexibility about execution.

People will play multiple roles within these dynamic organizations of the future. Leaders will morph into followers as the projects change, then morph back into leaders again. Organizations will encourage and reward this kind of behavior. The boundaries of the organization will be more

TABLE 1.3 Full-Spectrum Thinking for Societies

From Categorical	Toward Full Spectrum
Focus on separate societies, countries, or cultures	Focus on a diverse range of cultures, values, and beliefs across different societies and cultures
Centralized governments	Distributed governance
Nationalism	Globalism and regionalism
Culture focused: us vs. them	Cross-culture focused: what we have in common
Power held by a few	Power shared by many
Isolated	Connected
Generational cohorts by age	A youthquake of young activists with digital savvy, global connectivity, and growing power

porous as people come and go. On special forces teams in the military, for example, people play multiple roles depending on the circumstances, while still applying their areas of expertise in varied ways.

Full-Spectrum Thinking about Society

What categories do societies and cultures use to describe their citizens? As diversity increases, demographic categories will break down, with many more people who categorize themselves as "other." When they are asked if they are members of a church, which used to be an easy question to answer, many people now say that they are "spiritual, but not religious." Comfortable categories are breaking down, and that makes some people uncomfortable. They want to know who is in and who is out. Table 1.3 shows the direction of change over the next decade.

As migration grows, negative stereotypes will abound and the need for full-spectrum thinking will grow. Some countries and cultures will cling to the comfortable categories of the past, but the future will require full-spectrum thinking and action.

Peter Drucker was a full-spectrum thinker without the digital tools that are now emerging. The tools for full-spectrum thinking will be so much better over the next decade, just as the need for full-spectrum thinking grows. Constraining categories will yield to full-spectrum thinking, but it won't be an easy shift.

Youthquake is one of the terms I've adopted for describing the young people who grew up with digital media and have very high expectations for the world around them. These young people will have the vision and the tools to think across full spectrums of possibility and make the world a better place. After the Parkland shooting in Florida, for example, high school students organized themselves quickly into a national movement for gun control action. These young people cannot be categorized as a cohort; they are way too diverse. They are truly different, but we don't yet know how different they will be as they become adults.

I write this entire book through the lens of foresight. If you read it now in 2020, full-spectrum thinking will give you an early advantage. Later, full-spectrum thinking will be a prerequisite to success.

CHAPTER 2

The Coercion of Categories

Please Don't Stamp Me with **Your** Label

OUR BRAINS LOVE TO PUT NEW EXPERIENCES IN OLD boxes. New experiences that don't fit our preconceptions make us uncomfortable, so we force fit them into a category we think we already understand—even if that old box may be more harmful than helpful. Unexamined assumptions cloud our brains. Labels lie and our brains are accomplices. The categories of the past have brought us to a dangerous place.

Labels are sometimes assigned by an outside authority. A physician can do a test, for example, and label your sore throat as either strep throat or not. Science is based on categories: periodic tables, species, quantum physics moving from particles to waves. As part of an analytic process, categories can bring details and thus knowledge. Full-spectrum thinking brings context, which is the source of perspective and wisdom.

Labels are fine for yes/no assessments, but not when there is a range of possibilities. A label implies more judgment and less possibility. Labels are often assigned with certainty.

Individuals, organizations, and societies can be labeled falsely.

The Spike Lee movie *BlacKkKlansman* is a biting moral tale about the flammable dangers of simplistic labeling by race or ethnicity. The movie is based on the true story of Ron Stallworth, an African American police officer in Colorado Springs who infiltrated the Ku Klux Klan in a way that sounds impossible, except that it actually happened.

The Ron Stallworth character in the movie (played by John David Washington) talks to Klan members over the phone as part of the infiltration. Ron is African American, so he cannot let them see him in person, but he is very good at using his voice to make the Klan believe that he is a white person.

Ron Stallworth teams with Flip Zimmerman (played in the movie by Adam Driver), who is the undercover officer who pretends to be the in-person version of Ron Stallworth as he and Ron infiltrate the local KKK chapter. Flip is of Jewish heritage, which is an important part of the story. Here is a vivid exchange that highlights the dangers of simplistic labeling:

FLIP ZIMMERMAN: Well, I'm not risking my life to prevent some rednecks from lighting a couple sticks on fire.

RON STALLWORTH: This is the job. What's your problem?

FLIP ZIMMERMAN: That's my problem. For you, it's a crusade. For me, it's a job. It's not personal, nor should it be.

RON STALLWORTH: Why haven't you bought into this?

FLIP ZIMMERMAN: Why should I?

RON STALLWORTH: Because you're Jewish, brother. The so-called chosen people. You've been passing for a WASP. White Anglo-Saxon Protestant, cherry pie, hot dog, white boy. It's what some light-skinned Black folks do. They pass for white. Doesn't that hatred you've been hearing the Klan say doesn't that piss you off?

FLIP ZIMMERMAN: Of course it does.

RON STALLWORTH: Then why you acting like you ain't got skin in the game, brother?

FLIP ZIMMERMAN: Rookie, that's my f...ing business.

RON STALLWORTH: It's our business.[1]

In *BlacKkKlansman*, labels and categories are used as weapons. Categories can kill: *our* category is better than *your* category, or *you* frighten *us*. You must be eliminated. Categories can be used to control and subjugate others at the cost of our own awareness and understanding. Categories coerce. Categories lack nuance. Categories corrode complex realities under the guise of explanation.

Categories and labels invite and excuse quick judgments. Categories seem to protect us from things we don't understand, but often it is a false sense of protection. When we categorize, we contain our thinking and stop exploring alternative views of what's really going on. We divide ourselves into echo chambers where we only hear voices with which we already agree. MSNBC and Fox News, in political reporting in the US, present different points of view, but very few people watch both.

Categories and generalizations make it easy to group others into simplistic categories like "immigrants." Fear and perceived threat are motivators. Polarized thinking is extreme categorical thinking.

The Roots of Categorizing Go Deep

Just after the 9/11 attacks on the World Trade Center, I—like so many others—went through an emotional and soul-searching period. On an impulse, I created a special bookshelf in my library for those books that gave me a warm feeling when I just glanced at them. Thomas Kuhn's 1962 book *The Structure of Scientific Revolutions*, which I had first read as a PhD student at Northwestern, is one of those books that is still on my sacred shelf.

Kuhn argued that paradigms shape scientific disciplines but can solidify into rigid categories that lock out new points of view. I realize now that Kuhn was nudging me toward the notion of full-spectrum thinking to imagine new paradigms of thought—beyond the categories that constrain us:

> Led by a new paradigm, scientists adopt new instruments and look in new places. Even more important, during revolutions scientists see new and different things when looking with familiar instruments in places they have looked before. It is rather as if the professional community has

suddenly been transported to another planet where familiar objects are seen in a different light and are joined by unfamiliar ones as well.[2]

Full-spectrum thinking helps us see familiar situations in unfamiliar ways.

A *Washington Post* review of the classic 1979 John Fowles book *The Tree* captures both the value of categories and the risks. Fowles argued that there is a "green man" in all of us that senses nature all around us, but categories can get in the way:

> It (*Green Man*) adopts as its central image the small, formal garden kept by Carl Linnaeus, the 18th-century originator of the international system for classifying plants and animals.... Influenced by Linnaeus, [a] great deal of science is devoted to...providing specific labels, explaining specific mechanisms and ecologies, in short for sorting and tidying what seems in the mass indistinguishable one from the other.... [This knowledge] destroys or curtails certain possibilities of seeing, apprehending and experiencing. And that is the bitter fruit from the tree of Uppsalan knowledge.[3]

The green man in all of us is not a categorical thinker. The key to John Fowles's writing, he feels, lies in his relationship with nature. He acknowledges the value of scientific categorization of nature, but he feels we've gotten badly out of balance. "Of course, there is a place for the scientific, or quasi-scientific, analysis of art, as there is (and far greater) for that of nature. But the danger, in both art and nature, is that all emphasis is placed on the created, not the creation."[4]

The artist and writer James Prosek[5] has been writing and painting beyond categorical views of nature for years. He describes the limitations he feels as an artist trying to understand the flow of nature, beginning with his fascination with fish:

> I began to understand that species were less static than the fathers of modern taxonomy—those like Carl Linnaeus—once believed. That nature was static and classifiable was an idea perpetuated by the natural history museum (repository for dead nature), the zoo (repository for

living nature), and the book (repository for thoughts and images related to nature). These mediums were all distillations of nature, what individuals of authority deemed an appropriate cross section to present to the public. None had adequately represented Nature—at once chaotic, multifarious, and interconnected.

We willingly accept the way people in the past have viewed and arranged the world. Does bowing to that authority prevent us from looking at things with a fresh perspective? Naming gives us the illusion that nature is fixed, but it is as fluid as the language used to describe it. It is a challenge of the artist (if no one else) to un-name and re-name the world to remind us that fresh perspectives exist.[6]

I am fascinated with James Prosek's art and writing. We began an e-mail correspondence as I was writing this book, and here is how James Prosek described his interests to me:

> My obsession with the topic of bounded thinking or box-like thinking began with a childhood passion for the beauty and diversity of the natural world. I come at this topic in part through biological classification, how and why humans try to categorize and name life forms. The process of naming nature involves fragmenting what is essentially an undivided evolutionary continuum....I think we do share common interests in wanting humans to think more fluidly. In order to do so we have to overcome an urge to reduce and simplify and fragment nature...methods that served us well in the past. But this is not easy.[7]

Full-spectrum thinking is about pattern recognition. It is a nonlinear process that opens our thinking beyond categories and established lines of thought.

Categorize with caution and don't categorize too soon.

Full-spectrum thinking certainly links to general systems theory and the work of people like Gregory Bateson and his books like *Steps to an Ecology of Mind* (1972) and *Mind and Nature* (1979). Nature immerses us in a nondual process that shows a way of thinking beyond categories and even beyond thinking itself. The best practicing scientists use categories but learn not to be deluded by them.

The historian Charles King writes eloquently about how rigid categories dominated our thoughts about race, sex, and class up until Columbia University professor Franz Boas and his students created the discipline of cultural anthropology:

> A little over a century ago, any educated person knew that the world worked in certain obvious ways. Humans were individuals, but each was also representative of a specific type, itself the summation of a distinct set of racial, national, and sexual characteristics. Each type was fated to be more or less intelligent, idle, rule-bound, or warlike....Immigrants tended to dilute a country's natural vigor and breed political extremism.... Criminals were born to a life beyond the law but might be reformed.... Your proper category was so obvious that it was not what *you* said it was but what *someone else*, the census enumerator—usually a white man—said it was....The century's earliest version of the *Oxford English Dictionary*, the concise edition published in 1911, contained no entries for *racism*, *colonialism*, or *homosexuality*.[8]

Franz Boas's renegade group of social scientists busted society out of some very dangerous categorical thinking about race, gender, and class. They created a new academic discipline that contributed to a broader-spectrum mindset.

How the Medical Community Now Talks about Autism

The medical community has successfully moved from labeling someone as "having autism" or "being autistic" to thinking of "autism spectrum disorders" or "autism spectrum conditions."[9] Full-spectrum thinking more accurately reflects what's really going on. While it is still a categorization to say someone is "on the spectrum," at least there is a wide range of variations—some more difficult to diagnose and treat than others.

Where I work in Silicon Valley, being on the spectrum is now viewed as both a feature and a bug. Being on the spectrum means having an alternative learning style that is not neurotypical but possibly beyond neurotypical in some domains.

Ironically, people on the spectrum are often deeply focused within categories of thought. Perspective, context, and understanding of relationships are often elusive for people on the spectrum, as I understand it. They have an extreme sense of detail and precision. Sometimes they have great ability to focus but difficulties in relaxing. They sometimes do not have a sense of what is appropriate in a given social situation. They sometimes have both clarity and certainty within a very narrow focus, which can give them incredible ability to work with detail—but this same narrow focus can be a debilitating constraint.

At Institute for the Future, I have seen people note "I'm on the spectrum" on resumes or in conversation, as testimony to having the ability to think differently from others. At IFTF, we value that ability, but we seek out full-spectrum thinking. Some people embrace being on the spectrum if it helps them understand their own identity and explain it to others. They also need to seek out work that matches their abilities to focus.

The enterprise software corporation SAP now has an Autism at Work program, for example, "helping adults on the autism spectrum flourish in IT roles, bringing an untapped talent pool into the workplace and fueling further innovation."[10] At UCLA and Stanford there is a PEERS clinic that provides a "manualized, social skills training intervention for youth with social challenges. It has a strong evidence-base for use with adolescents and young adults with autism spectrum disorder."[11] A similar program at Xavier University is called The X-Path Program.[12]

In the fall of 2018, Kent State University signed the first Division 1 basketball player on the autism spectrum to a full basketball scholarship. Kalin Bennett had multiple basketball scholarship offers but chose Kent State because of the resources it has to engage with people on the autism spectrum. Here's how he describes his goals: "I want to make an impact not just on the court, but with kids that are struggling with the same things I am.... I want to let them know, hey, if I can do this, you can do it, too. A lot of times they feel alone and by themselves, and I felt that same way growing up."[13]

"He is really a phenomenal human being," said Gina Campana, Kent State's assistant director of the Autism Initiative for Research, Education and Outreach. "A light emanates from this young man. We're going to be lucky to get him at Kent State."[14]

At a young age, Bennett's family was told he might never function with others, because of his autism, but through therapy he was able to overcome those obstacles. "I showed him his [medical] file. I wanted him to read this book of files so he would know how he needs to always keep fighting," Bennett's mother, Sonja, told Cleveland.com. As an 18-year-old, he revisited the therapist who gave him the initial diagnosis that turned out to be so wrong. His mother described the meeting: "So, when he read it, and then met the therapist, he said; 'Are you the one who said I would never do this and never do that?' She said, 'Yes Kalin, I am.' He said, 'My question is, I hope you haven't told anybody else that because you could ruin their lives.'"[15]

In the future, I believe that perception of and engagement with people who are on the spectrum will move from disease to learning style, bug to feature, medication alone to prescribed gaming experiences for treatment. Still, some people on the spectrum will be deeply constrained by categorical thinking and will have difficulty moving beyond the categories where they can function well.

About five years ago, I met a game designer named Lat Ware in Silicon Valley. He told me his poignant story of being diagnosed at age five with ADHD[16] and being given medications that made him sick and suicidal at times. Remarkably, he designed a video game that improved his ADHD symptoms. His game, called Throw Trucks with Your Mind, uses a low-cost headset that reads the player's brain activity into a video game to give the player telekinetic superpowers controlled in the game and on the screen by the player's own thoughts. The game reads spikes in the player's brain's beta waves and translates them into proportional telekinetic force. In the game, you have the feeling of literally throwing trucks with your brain. In the future, I believe that doctors will prescribe video games for treatment of some conditions such as ADHD, sleep problems, depression, addiction, and concussion recovery. Lat Ware is now the founder of Crooked Tree Studios, a company pioneering in the packaging of traditional neurofeedback therapy in the context of competitive video games for all ages.

Labels are particularly dangerous in health care. I was speaking at the Academy of Integrative Health & Medicine (AIHM) conference in 2018, and the speaker after me was Scott Shannon, MD, who wrote a book with a title that I found telling: *Please Don't Label My Child: Break the Doctor-Diagnosis-Drug*

Cycle and Discover Safe, Effective Choices for Your Child's Emotional Health.[17] Physicians, especially in time-constrained visits, often make quick judgments, and people can get labeled in destructive ways. Some people do want to use labels to establish their identities, but many people don't want others to label them. When in doubt, don't label unless someone labels themself first. On the other hand, insurance companies require physicians to put conditions into categories in order to get paid.

Health care is gradually shifting from categorical toward more holistic full-spectrum thinking. Medical students, for example, have traditionally been sharply categorized by their year in medical school (think *first year, second year, intern,* etc.). Now competency-based assessments show that different students perform at different competency levels—regardless of their year in medical school. Computers are much better at categorizing than humans, but humans have the ability to think in relationships and patterns. Humans can juggle the objective with the associative with much more grace than computers.

"Inpatient" and "outpatient" are two more sharp medical categories that are yielding to a continuum of care. Care providers used to have focused jobs with titles like "preop," where now there is a spectrum of jobs, roles, and functions relating to the needs of the patients matched to the skills of the care providers. Where care providers were often caught in lockstep categories, they now seek out the clarity of a spectrum of care based on patient needs. The lesson is clear: categorize with caution and consider a full spectrum of options when you can.

The Politics of Careless Categorizing

I met Amy Chua when we were both speaking for a McKinsey directors conference some years ago in Istanbul. Amy Chua is a law professor at Yale, the author of the book *Battle Hymn of the Tiger Mother,* and a student of political tribes. Her book *Political Tribes: Group Instinct and the Fate of Nations* takes a deep look at the dangers of simplistic tribal categorization:

> When groups feel threatened, they retreat into tribalism. They close
> ranks and become more insular, more defensive, more punitive, more

us-versus-them. In America today, every group feels this way to some extent.[18]

The overarching identity of the United States of America is threatened by political tribes that have no interest in choosing to do things together. As reviewer David Frum commented when Chua's book came out: "Worsening social divisions are much easier to exploit than to explain or redress."[19] Polarized thinking leads to tribal warfare much more often than it leads to forgiveness and reconciliation. Tribes are not necessarily bad. In some regions of the world, particularly in parts of Africa, tribes are built into the social fabric in very constructive ways. What I'm talking about here is rigid tribalism such as what Amy Chua describes as breaking out in the United States. In a world of tribal thinking, people—especially kids on the verge of becoming adults—naturally ask, What tribe am I in?

Full-spectrum thinking will be a technology-enabled antidote to mindless labeling, as well as polarized tribal thinking. Full-spectrum thinking will allow people to leapfrog barriers like thoughtless and limited stereotyping of new experiences and of new people who seem or appear different. We often think we're categorizing definitively when we're only categorizing approximately at best. Full-spectrum thinking will help us find common ground across differences.

There is an interesting argument being made that most Americans aren't actually very polarized—in spite of the popular view that we are. Perhaps we are already becoming full-spectrum thinkers, even though the mass media makes us think that we are polarized and often gives airtime to the most polarizing groups. A recent study called Hidden Tribes of America surveyed a statistically representative sample of Americans. Using focus groups, one-on-one interviews, and written surveys, the authors of the surveys set out to answer the question How divided is the US public? Are we in fact so divided, as today's media has led us to believe, that we can no longer find common ground among each other?

The research concluded that there is still an underlying agreement and common ground among the majority of Americans. Issues that are portrayed as deeply polarized (immigration, establishing a pathway to citizenship for DACA students, racism, or the overuse of political correctness) are in fact not so widely dissimilar. The researchers conclude that more than 75 percent of Americans believe our political differences aren't so great that we still can't work together to find adequate solutions. "America is so much more than two tribes," and our differences are not in fact so great that we cannot come together once more.[20]

Perhaps Americans are more on a spectrum—and less divided—than the popular press would lead us to believe. Of course, this conclusion doesn't matter if most Americans believe that they are polarized, even if they are not. If people feel polarized, that may be more influential than the scientific results of a survey that says they are not. Part of the challenge is that we don't have good language for working together across our firmly held categories of thought.

Full-spectrum thinking will help us realize that we are in fact not as polarized as we think we are. Even if we are polarized, our perceptions of tribalism may be more powerful than the reality.

As I was writing this book, our grandsons visited and I got to read my favorite Berenstain Bear books to them, as I had to our children before them. The wisdom of Berenstain Bears comes through as Mama Bear tries to break Sister Bear of her bad habit of chewing her fingernails down to the nubbins.[21]

> "A habit," Mama said as she pushed the wheelbarrow along the well-worn path, "is something you do so often you don't even have to think about it. Habits are a very important part of our lives. And most of them are good—like brushing your teeth and combing your fur when you get up in the morning, and looking both ways before you cross a road. But some habits aren't so good…it's sort of like this path. I've wheeled this barrow over it so many times that it has worn a deep rut right down the middle. And it keeps getting deeper every time I use it. Why, it's so deep now that I can't get out of it without a little help. That's the way it is with a bad habit—the more you use it, the harder it is to get out of it."[22]

Rigid categorical thinking is a bad habit we need to break. In this chapter, we have discussed the past limitations of classifying nature, diagnosing medical conditions like autism, and the polarization of today's political tribes. In the past, categories have been useful at times—but they are also coercive. Categories won't go away, but we have to learn how to use them less often and more cautiously.

When we are frightened, categories can help calm us down. Comfortable categories are very useful, for example, at 3 a.m. when you are half asleep, half awake, and fully frightened. Categorizing, generalizing, and labeling are dangerous, however. We cannot go on categorizing as we have in the past. Fortunately, futures thinking can help us escape the boxes of the past and present.

CHAPTER 3

Escape the Boxes of the Past

How to Use Futures Thinking

THIS IS THE MOST FRIGHTENING 10-YEAR FORECAST I'VE ever done, but it is also the most hopeful—and I've been saying that for the last 10 years. The scramble will be beyond many people's ability to cope.

The scramble will reward clarity (being very clear about where you want to go, but very flexible about how you get there), but it will punish certainty. There will be very little true certainty in a scramble, but there will be lots of false certainty.

As the scramble increases, the value of full-spectrum thinking will increase. Unfortunately, the temptations of false or simplistic categorization will also grow.

Since 9/11, I've been using *VUCA* (volatile, uncertain, complex, and ambiguous) as an umbrella term to describe the future world.[1] Inspired by my experiences with the Army War College, I created what I call the positive VUCA: *volatility* yields to *vision, uncertainty* yields to *understanding, complexity* yields to *clarity*, and *ambiguity* yields to *agility*. Both the negative and the positive VUCA will be basic to life in the future. For many people I've worked with, VUCA has been a very useful concept to open a conversation about alternative futures.

In this book, I use the words *scramble* and *VUCA* interchangeably to set context and expectations for the future. Whatever name you choose to give it, the future will stretch whatever categories we create to describe it. It will require full-spectrum thinking.

The scramble will certainly be a VUCA world, and the Army is a lot more ready for it than the rest of us. But I have found that *VUCA* can be confusing or off-putting for some people. The term *scramble* seems more straightforward and immediately understandable without introducing an acronym or an unfamiliar word.

Futurist Peter Schwartz suggested in 1991 that we all need to develop what he called elegantly "the art of the long view."[2]

If you look long, gradients of possibility shine through. Baby-stepping from the present toward the future doesn't work nearly as well as leaping out and looking back. The present is so noisy that it is very difficult to listen for the future. It is so easy to get stuck in categories of thought that are grounded in the past but ignorant of the future.

The philosopher Søren Kirkegaard said:

Life can only be understood backwards;
but it must be lived forwards.[3]

I first read Kirkegaard when I was in divinity school, and I've always been drawn to his thought. It is meaningful to me that the elite strategy consultancy Innosight (founded by Clayton Christensen and Mark Johnson) uses this Kirkegaard quote on their website and points out that future-back visioning is a process aimed at overcoming this basic dilemma of life and living. Innosight goes on to use the metaphor of planning a trip. Let's say you're traveling from San Francisco to London. It makes much more sense to plan according to your destination than your starting point, but many organizations plan from where they are, informed mostly by where they have been.

Since the early 1970s, I've been living my life focused 10 years ahead, working backward to understand choices in the present. I am not an expert in the present, but I've gotten pretty good at sensing where things are going.

When I first got into the futures field, the focus was on event prediction. Now, prediction is for the amateurs who don't know better, and the futures field is focused on sense-making. Humility is back in fashion, but so is activism. Now, people want to make the future, not just hear about it. Making the future in the next decade is going to be particularly tricky.

Foresight to Insight to Action

At Institute for the Future, we use our own Foresight-Insight-Action model to keep us oriented. I first published this model in my 2007 book called *Get There Early: Sensing the Future to Compete in the Present,*[4] and we use it now on almost every project as a core discipline of futures thinking. Figure 3.1 shows my most recent update of this model.

This model can be used to generate full-spectrum thinking about the past, present, and future. It is a flywheel for spinning out possibilities.

The cycle begins with a cautionary note about prediction. The goal of futures thinking is not to predict. The future is unpredictable. The way to evaluate a futurist is not to ask if the forecasted future actually happened. That's the way you evaluate a fortune-teller. The way to evaluate a futurist is to ask if the forecasted future provoked insight and action. A good forecast should lead to better strategy and more informed action. The goal of a forecast is to provoke, not to predict.

Sometimes, however, the word *forecast* can get in the way. For some, a forecast is a prediction. A sales forecast, for example, is often a quantitative prediction of sales during a designated reporting period. When we did a custom forecast in Western Europe, we ran into this language difference. In that case, we use the word *outlook* instead of *forecast.* For me, a forecast is a plausible, internally consistent story about the future that is designed to provoke insight and action. Once we do a base forecast, we often do scenarios off the base. You can certainly use another word for "forecast," if it communicates better in a particular environment.

The best forecasts are often the ones you don't like. My IFTF colleague Jamais Cascio argues that the best forecasts are those that are usefully wrong. Forecasts like this are successful if they don't happen, or if they allow you to see things you didn't see before.

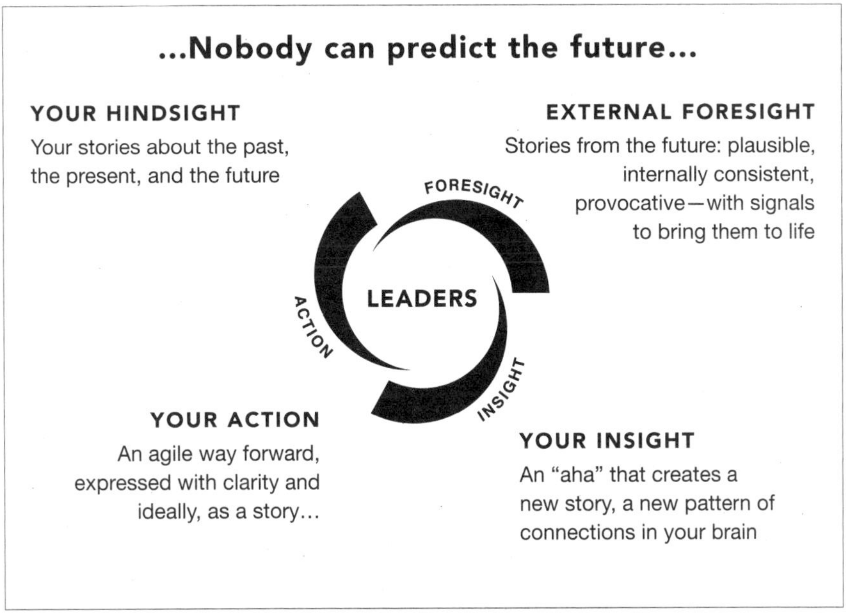

...Nobody can predict the future...

YOUR HINDSIGHT
Your stories about the past,
the present, and the future

EXTERNAL FORESIGHT
Stories from the future: plausible,
internally consistent,
provocative—with signals
to bring them to life

FORESIGHT

LEADERS

ACTION

INSIGHT

YOUR ACTION
An agile way forward,
expressed with clarity and
ideally, as a story...

YOUR INSIGHT
An "aha" that creates a
new story, a new pattern of
connections in your brain

FIGURE 3.1: Institute for the Future's Foresight-Insight-Action model.

Full-spectrum thinking lives between hindsight and foresight; it empowers our ability to imagine a range of alternative futures.

"The future is already here, it's just unevenly distributed" said novelist William Gibson. At Institute for the Future, we call these unevenly distributed futures *signals* of change, and they help bring foresight to life. Compelling and provocative signals are particularly powerful because they change the way we think. After experiencing the most powerful signals, we can't go back to our old ways of thinking.[5] Signals bring foresight to life. I will be introducing signals frequently throughout the book.

Whether we like it or not, foresight always starts with hindsight. Our brains all have what neuroscientists call a "personal neural story net" that helps us process what's going on and try to predict what will happen next. Unfortunately, many leaders have personal neural story nets that are dominated by a kind of "we tried it and it didn't work" assumption set that is hard to crack.

Foresight attempts to break into your personal neural story nets with a new story of possibility that is plausible, internally consistent, and provocative. The best forecasts have a bite to them. They are provocative, without turning people off. They are familiar enough to be understandable but don't sound like the same old thing.

Foresight should always acknowledge the importance of hindsight. When we do 10-year forecasts at IFTF, we typically look at least 50 years back. A 60-year swath of time is about right for most business forecasting, in our experience. It is important to look even farther back than we are looking ahead. Once, for a forecast of green health, IFTF looked 200 years back because of the long traditions of natural healing.

At Institute for the Future, our executive director, Marina Gorbis, has been encouraging people to expand their temporal bandwidth, looking back as well as looking forward in order to understand the larger patterns of change. Unfortunately, studying history is becoming the purview of elite colleges and very motivated individuals since mainstream education is focused so early on job-related skills. A different kind of inequality is emerging. As Eric Alterman has noted:

> Inequality affects our physical and mental health, our ability to get along with one another and to make our voices heard and our political system accountable, and, of course, the futures that we can offer our children. Lately, I've noticed a feature of economic inequality that has not received the attention it deserves. I call it "intellectual inequality."
>
> I do not refer to the obvious and ineluctable fact that some people are smarter than others but, rather, to the fact that some people have the resources to try to understand our society while most do not.[6]

The long view can be a competitive advantage, but you may not see the impacts right away. I was involved in a military forecasting exercise recently that focused on China. From what I gathered in those conversations, the Chinese People's Party is thinking way ahead, perhaps as far out as 200 years ahead. As I understand it, this is not predictive forecasting or planning but rather an effort to set long-term goals, do scenario planning on distant horizons, and then work backward to figure out how to get from the present to their desired future. I believe that it will be a competitive advantage for China.

Compare China's long-term view to that of the US government, where there is very little thought about the long-term future. Our military is planning 10 to 20 years ahead, and our health and health care agencies definitely have long-term efforts under way on about that horizon or a bit farther. From 1972 to 1995 the US Congress had the Office of Technology Assessment to provide Congressional members and committees with objective and authoritative analysis of futures content from all around the world. Princeton University still hosts the OTA legacy site, but there is no current effort to provide foresight for Congress. Sadly, in this polarized political world, most elected officials seem to have little interest in the long-term future. They are often certain but rarely clear.

Now, FUTURE, Next

Most companies we work with have a strategic orientation that can be summarized as Now, Next, Future—or sometimes Horizon 1, Horizon 2, Horizon 3.[7] Most of the energy goes into Now or Horizon 1, as it should. Next or Horizon 2 gets some attention, usually thinking ahead just a few years. Future or Horizon 3 is often a catchall for interesting new ideas and possibilities. Typically, Future is nobody's job and it really doesn't get much attention. For many companies, the "future" is just a few years ahead— rarely is it 10 or more years ahead. That needs to change if companies are to thrive in the scramble.

In my 2017 book *The New Leadership Literacies: Thriving in a Future of Extreme Disruption and Distributed Everything,*[8] the core new leadership literacy is the ability to look back from the future but act now. Mark Johnson and his colleagues at Innosight call this "future-back visioning" or "future-back strategy."[9] Present-forward strategy is just too difficult and dangerous in a world where the present is so noisy.

Ten years ahead, for example, sensors will be everywhere. They will be very cheap, many of them will be connected, and some of them will be in or on our bodies. What's not obvious is just how sensors will spread and who will make money from the process.

Learning from the Foresight-Insight-Action model, it is possible to make one small change in *order* that will result in a very large change in *impact.* Instead of Foresight to Insight to Action, start from Action, then leap out to

Foresight, and *then* come back to Insight for strategy and innovation. Many companies we work with already use a Now, Next, Future framework. But when facing a highly uncertain future, a scramble, you will need to use strategic foresight to think like this:

1. Now   2. FUTURE   3. Next

Horizon 1   Horizon 3   Horizon 2

It is completely appropriate to spend most of your time on the Now, the Action. That is where your business is, and that's where you should focus. Incremental innovation is great, as long as it keeps getting results. If you invest in Future—not just Next—you will be able to achieve much greater clarity. Clarity emerges in the space between insight and action. You want to be very clear about where you are going, but very flexible about how you get there.

In 2008, Dow Chemical participated in an IFTF project for the Global Environmental Management Initiative (GEMI) that delivered a custom forecast on the external future forces likely to disrupt the concept of sustainability in business. One of the key forecast findings was a growing imperative for looking long. Mark Weick from Dow described how that 2008 forecast encouraged his company to take an even longer view in their own future:

> In 2009, Dow found value in looking out at the year 2097 to create what we called the "Dow@200 Vision." The year 2097 was an iconic year for Dow—since Dow started in 1897, the year 2097 represents Dow's 200th birthday. The value in reaching so far out into the future was two-fold. First, no matter how much talent and effort we could put into keeping the existing manufacturing assets running, looking at 2097 meant that every existing manufacturing plant, every process, and every business model would had to have been recreated and recapitalized during that time frame. What decisions did we make over those decades to get to a sustainable company in a sustainable society with sustainable business models?
>
> Second, we had to project that even our youngest employees would be dead. This time frame forced us to look a few generations beyond ourselves and think about the legacy we would leave. We spent a few months looking out that far, and then resumed a shorter-term view—the next 5 to 20 years—to think about the next steps that we should take. This

process finally resulted in the April 2015 launch of Dow's current 2025 Sustainability Goals.[10]

Recognizing that investments like a new plant have a life of 30 or 40 years, Dow shifted the "third horizon" in their major planning process to be 100 years out. Working with IFTF encouraged them to think ahead 100 years and be disciplined to imagine the 100-year cycle of long-term initiatives.

Though 10-year forecasting is easier than 1-year or 2-year forecasting, you must look beyond 10 years to get the best view. The future is not always incremental, and it is often disruptive. Trends are patterns of change you can anticipate with confidence, but disruptions are *breaks* in the pattern of change. Looking long can help you get a better view of where things are going.

Steven Johnson, the wonderful technology sense-maker, describes the need for engaging with the future by using an analogy from the world of sound:

> Complex decisions require full-spectrum analysis. Imagine the many scales of human experience as slices of the frequency spectrum of audible sound. When we adjust the EQ of a recording, we are zooming in on one of those slices; we want to turn the low end down a bit so the bass doesn't rumble, or boost the midrange so we can hear the vocals. Music producers have surgically precise tools that allow them to target astonishingly narrow slices of that spectrum, tools that let you extract the background hum of a 120 Hz electric current from a mix, but nothing else.... Decisions can be imagined in a similar way.[11]

The most useful foresight provokes a new pattern of thinking in your brain, a kind of Aha! that you experience viscerally. Provocative foresight erupts into your personal neural story net and sparks new stories. You don't need to agree with a forecast to be provoked by it.

From Futures Thinking to Full-Spectrum Thinking

Figure 3.2 shows how I apply the Foresight-Insight-Action model to full-spectrum thinking.

HINDSIGHT about CATEGORIES

Challenge unexamined assumptions about yourself, others, organizations, and societies

FULL-SPECTRUM FORESIGHT

Imagine new opportunities across gradients of possibility

FULL-SPECTRUM ACTION

Create an agile way forward that **transcends** the categories of the past

FULL-SPECTRUM INSIGHT

Strive for an "aha" that creates **a new spectrum of possibility**, a new pattern of connections in your brain

FIGURE 3.2: Full-spectrum thinking as a mix of hindsight, foresight, insight, and action.

It is tempting to argue with any forecast, and you always can argue, since the future is unpredictable. The art of using foresight is to accept a forecast as plausible, internally consistent, and provocative. Then, allow yourself to be provoked by it. If you don't think a forecast is clear enough for you, develop alternative forecasts or scenarios.

At IFTF, after we complete a forecast, we like to challenge ourselves by doing a forecast where the opposite of what we think will happen happens. One of my favorite corporate clients always asked us to do that at the end of a forecast. Most clients and most futurists, unfortunately, do not do this kind of alternative future forecasting to challenge and exercise their best base forecast.

The ultimate evaluation of a forecast is whether or not it provokes a better decision in the present. Strategy lives between insight and action. Willie Pietersen at Columbia Business School teaches that every good strategy is based on a compelling insight.[12] It turns out that foresight is a very good way to provoke insight—even if you don't agree with the forecast.

My colleague Jeremy Kirshbaum taught me the importance of action that provokes foresight. Jeremy works on new innovations involving both Africa and China. He calls the geographies where he works "high delta" because of the speed of the change. His point is that action in these fast-moving areas yields new insight about the future, not just about what works in the present. This observation is very consistent with the Silicon Valley mantra to fail early, fail often, and fail cheaply. Jeremy's insight is that rapid prototyping leads not only to success in the present, but also to a new ability to forecast the future.

A Future view will reveal your options much more clearly. Next is still way too noisy and is often overshadowed by the Now. Most people and most organizations should invest most of their time where the Action is but regularly turn to Foresight and Insight.

In the summer of 2018, the Institute for the Future was asked to do a custom 10-year forecast for Southern New Hampshire University (SNHU). I had never heard of them before their board of directors came to spend a day with us in Silicon Valley. Their story explains why the future will demand full-spectrum thinking and also how they are being rewarded for their innovative efforts to provide affordable education on a global scale. I now believe SNHU is a signal for the future.

A little more than a decade before they visited IFTF in 2018, SNHU was a small liberal arts college of about 3,000 students in Manchester, New Hampshire, that was struggling to survive—like so many other educational institutions. Through a series of bold moves, SNHU has evolved into a thriving online and in-person global learning community. They were already well into this transformation when we started to work with them, but they asked us to look 10 years ahead to the college student of the year 2030.

This custom forecast revealed a future that will require us all to move beyond narrow categorical thinking. An IFTF research team led by my colleague Kathi Vian identified external future forces that are most likely to disrupt the college student of 2030. A future force is a pattern of change that is likely to disrupt today's way of doing things. Future forces can result from innovations in technologies, policies, markets, and cultures. Such patterns of change challenge us to think beyond today's best practices and create new ways of engaging with tomorrow. The value of college or graduate degrees will be called into question. Are they worth the time and money? For what return? And the student loan debt hanging over many of today's students and parents is not sustainable.

Scrambling with Three Big External Future Forces

Drawing from our forecast of the college student of 2030, here are the external future forces that will collide to create a future that will require and reward full-spectrum thinking—but punish categorical thinking. The learning resources in this world will multiply.

A future force is an external wave of change so large that it is difficult to imagine much you can do about it. With robust futures thinking, you can at least decide whether or not you want to ride that wave of change. And, with luck, you may be able to at least avoid getting hit by it. A future force is a forecast, a plausible, internally consistent provocative view of what we think will happen. It is designed to provoke insight and action by others, not to predict the future. From a base forecast, it is best to do alternative scenarios. Even in highly uncertain times, it is usually possible to at least forecast direction of change.

I believe that three external future forces will be particularly pressing over the next decade—and all will require full-spectrum thinking. These future forces are at the root of the increasingly intense scramble that we will be facing. All three started in the past, are becoming critical in the present, and will get much worse in the future. These forces will scramble the next decade, and they will demand futures thinking in general and full-spectrum thinking in particular.

These forces cannot be solved within the categories of the past. In fact, the categories of the past have exacerbated these future forces and made them even worse. These future forces are deeply rooted in the trends of the past, but they are also breaking into the patterns of change.

The growing asset gap between the rich and the poor will, in very tangible but complicated ways, threaten the world.

Even as the world becomes more connected, it will become more fragmented and polarized—largely driven by stark rich-poor gaps that will be increasingly visible. Very poor individuals—watch out in particular for young people who are poor and lack hope—will see the very rich, sometimes in high definition. What we used to call the "digital divide" will become a lot more complicated. Rich people will still have access to better connectivity and better digital tools, but poor people will be much more connected globally. It is hard to do a forecast of the rich-poor gap in which things get better over the next decade, and it's easy to do a forecast in which they get worse.

The columnist Thomas L. Friedman wrote a summer 2019 column called "The Answers to Our Problems Aren't as Simple as Left or Right: The Old Binary Choices No Longer Work." He quotes Marina Gorbis as saying "the answer is not socialism or abandoning markets, but a vibrant state that can use taxes and regulations to reshape markets in ways that divide the pie, grow the pie, and create more public wealth—mass transit, schools, parks, scholarships, libraries, and basic scientific research—so that more individuals, start-ups, and communities have more tools to adapt and thrive." Friedman ends his analysis by observing that "the real solutions require a left-wing wrench, a right-wing hammer, and all sorts of new tools and combinations we've never imagined."

In his travels, Friedman sees hope in local communities even as the national and global debate continues in such a polarized fashion. He ends with this: "Leave your rigid right-left grid on the hook outside the door. That's actually happening locally. But taking that national is really hard."[13]

Marina Gorbis added this in a July 24, 2019, e-mail to IFTF staff: "We need to leverage the power of the state to shape direction of private investment to pro-social ends while ensuring more equitable distribution of economic returns in the population." This is thinking with a broad spectrum of possibility.

In 2014, the French economist Thomas Piketty published the remarkable book called *Capital in the Twenty-first Century*.[14] Piketty became an instant celebrity in many business circles, and he prompted serious conversation about the rich-poor gap. His historical analysis showed that the rich-poor gap is deeply rooted in history and that the asset gap is growing faster than increases in wages. Market forces alone, Piketty warns, are not likely to decrease the asset gap, and in the current global political climate, government policies to close the gap are unlikely.

The sure thing is that the rich-poor gap will get increasingly visible and flammable. When rich kids flaunt their wealth, it will be like throwing matches on dry tinder. Futures literacy will improve, particularly among the kids. The true digital natives, who I will discuss in Chapter 6, will be much more comfortable and empowered in this future world—if they have hope.

Cyber terrorism and shape-shifting criminal networks will disrupt individual, organizational, and societal life.

Asymmetric warfare has become a fact of life, and it will become more common in the future. Very small groups of people with extremely disruptive views will be able to find each other and do bad things that will be amplified through digital networks. Finding and stopping these deviant acts will be a constant dilemma of peacekeeping. The trade-offs between privacy and the hope of protection from terrorism will intensify. The new digital tools will help very good people, but they will also be there for very bad people. And the very bad people won't have the legal constraints that law-abiding citizens will have.

Sean McFate's book *The New Rules of War* introduces the new term *durable disorder* to describe the foreseeable future:

> The twenty-first century is maturing into a world mired in perpetual chaos, with no way to contain it.... This growing entropy signifies the emergence of a new global system that I call "durable disorder," which contains rather than solves problems. This condition will define the coming age.... Wars will be fought mostly in the shadows by covert means, and plausible deniability will prove more effective than firepower in an information age.... Conflicts will not start and stop, but will grind on in "forever wars."[15]

McFate uses the term *durable disorder* in much the same way that I use *VUCA world* or *scramble*.

The disruption of global intelligence systems—with processing speeds that far outpace human processing, vast stores of data that would overwhelm human minds, and globally connected sensors that track the physical world—will challenge learners, workers, and managers of organizations to develop finely honed skills in human–machine collaboration. Even though we will all be augmented in some way, computers will only rarely replace people one to one. Rather, as Professor Thomas W. Malone at MIT suggests, we will be in a world of "superminds."[16] Unfortunately, some of the most powerful superminds will be criminals who will operate outside the laws that the rest of us will be following.

For example, University of Chicago historian Kathleen Belew studies the white power movement in the United States and has concluded that "war is not neatly contained in the space and time legitimated by the state. It reverberates in other terrains and lasts long past armistice. It comes home in ways bloody and unexpected."[17] The white power movement is heavily invested in the category of white heritage and is willing to fight to retain white status and avoid what they see as replacement of whites with others.

Over the next decade asymmetrical warfare and criminal activities will become both more destructive and more difficult to control. Hybrid warfare is particularly troubling, where mercenaries and criminal networks—many of whom don't officially exist—disrupt in any way possible. In some cases, disruption itself will be the goal.

**Global climate disruption will cause havoc sooner
and more severely than most people anticipate.**

Some futures are looming over us whether we are paying attention or not. Even though it is easier to look long than it is to make sense out of the noisy present, that doesn't mean that we will necessarily do anything about it. The Institute for the Future did its first forecast of global climate disruption in 1977. It was a panel study of the world's leading experts. IFTF is an independent nonprofit and not an advocacy group, but we have done periodic studies since 1977, and it has become obvious that global climate disruption is real, with the only question being whose models you believe about how bad it will become how soon. Somehow as a planet, we must cycle our thinking from Foresight to Insight to Action so an awful future doesn't happen.

This tweet from William Gibson in 2018 makes the need for future-back thinking clear: "All imagined futures lacking recognition of anthropogenic climate-change will increasingly seem absurdly shortsighted. Virtually the entire genre will be seen to have utterly missed the single most important thing we were doing with technology."[18] Our children and especially our grandchildren will ask: What were those leaders thinking? Where were the futurists? In the present world, we are infected by short-termism.

Vanderbilt professor Amanda Little's book called *The Fate of Food* explores links between climate disruption and food supply. In this interview before the book came out, she highlights the need for full-spectrum thinking to be applied to how we think about food and technology:

> There's a deep distrust of technology as applied to food—understandably, because industrial agriculture is so flawed. But as someone observing this debate for years, I wondered: Why must it be so binary? We need a synthesis of the two approaches.
>
> We need a "third way" that borrows from the wisdom of traditional food production and from our most advanced technologies. Such an approach would allow us to grow more and higher-quality food while restoring, rather than degrading, public health and the environment.[19]

We are way beyond yes/no choices in deciding what mix of technology and food makes the most sense, for whom. Technology will be required, but there is a wide spectrum of options for how it might be used.

This chapter introduced the tools of future thinking that will be required to do robust full-spectrum thinking. In addition, I described the three external future forces that we have inherited from the past but that will be particularly disturbing over the next decade. The Foresight-Insight-Action model will be applied throughout the book, as will a Now, FUTURE, Next way of thinking and acting. The long view will make it easier to assess choices in the present. I believe that these future forces will be most disruptive and most in need of broader analysis.

Full-spectrum thinking will require discipline and sophisticated use of digital tools, networks, and engagement with a next generation of leaders. Part Two introduces the new tools, the new networks, and the true digital natives who will bring full-spectrum thinking to life.

PART TWO

NEW FULL-SPECTRUM TOOLS, NETWORKS, AND PEOPLE

THE SCRAMBLE OF TODAY'S WORLD IS VERY DIFFICULT TO understand, and it will be impossible to unscramble. We will need a full-spectrum mindset to have any hint of what is going on, because the scramble will get even worse in the future. The three external future forces that I introduced at the end of Chapter 3 will create crises of trust, control, and relationship with underlying social order. Part Two will introduce the fresh mix of tools, connectivity, and people who will make full-spectrum thinking possible in new ways first—then make full-spectrum thinking mandatory.

Fortunately, digital media will improve our ability to sense what is going on around us. There is also a next generation of digital natives who know how to utilize these digital media in more sophisticated ways than their elders.

Most of these emerging tools and network resources have been around a long time, but they haven't yet scaled in the ways that will become possible over the next decade. What's coming is a new mix of old and new that will create a much more robust toolset.

Chapter 4
Clarity Filters
Scrambling with Distrust

Just as the present scramble is increasing and the need becomes more urgent, the networks for full-spectrum thinking are becoming more powerful, more available, and much easier to use. Full-spectrum thinking is intellectually demanding, but big data analytics, visualization, and gameful engagement will make it much easier to practice.

Chapter 5
Distributed-Authority Networks
Scrambling for Control

Next-generation networks and connectivity will enhance our ability to see, understand, and even embody full spectrums of possibility. These tools will allow us to see new patterns and seek new clarity.

Chapter 6
The True Digital Natives
Scrambling with the Social Order

The digital natives, who started to become adults in 2010 or later, are now young adults who will transform the workplace and life. I'm very optimistic about these young people, *if* they have hope. A full-spectrum mindset and full-spectrum thinking will amplify hope by helping us imagine new possibilities.

The true digital natives will be much better prepared for full-spectrum thinking than the rest of us. The digital natives will transform the workplace. Full-spectrum thinking comes much more easily to them since they grew up with digital tools and media. Young people—especially the youthquake of digital natives who are 24 or younger in 2020—will understand and accept full-spectrum thinking much better than the adults. It will help them find their vision, their voice, and their ways of making a living.

Kids are born with an ability to think expansively about the world around them, until we categorize and test it out of them. Full-spectrum thinking will help the kids and the rest of us figure out how to make the future a better place.

Priority Questions for Part Two

As an individual, how can you learn to use today's current and tomorrow's emerging digital tools and networks to help you engage with complexity in constructive ways right now?

As an organization, how do you design and implement digital tools and networks today, to support full-spectrum thinking and resist simplistic categorization?

How can societies regulate—without overregulating—emerging digital media and networks in such a way that they encourage diverse thought and avoid unfair categorization?

For older individuals, organizations, and society right now, how can you welcome and engage with natives who have advanced digital experience? How can you encourage cross-generational mentoring?

CHAPTER 4

Clarity Filters

Scrambling with Distrust

IN 2018, A SILICON VALLEY START-UP CALLED SOAPAI developed one of the first digital clarity filters to help young people decide what is fake news and what is not. Whether or not SoapAI succeeds commercially, I expect that it is a signal of the new wave of clarity filters to come over the next decade. Later in this chapter, I will talk more about SoapAI as an early probe for what's next.

These kinds of systems will help people make sense out of the emerging future. I expect clarity filters to be a very competitive space, fueled by technology tools that have been around a long time (like AI and machine learning) but are finally becoming practical and scalable.

While the term *clarity filter* may be unfamiliar, clarity filtering is ancient. The village elder was a clarity filter, as were shamans, priests, and other voices of authority who people trusted to help them make sense out of the world around them. Today, our own personal medical doctors often play the role of clarity filters to help us treat illness and make healthy choices.

Clarity filters are trusted sense-makers.

Martin Luther King Jr., for example, was a clarity filter. I attended the same divinity school as Dr. King, Crozer Theological Seminary, and I was studying there when he was killed. The community was shocked. One of the responses by Crozer was a new course on the life and thought of Martin Luther King. The syllabus was designed to re-create the intellectual influences that were most important to Dr. King when he was in divinity school,[1] and the class was taught by one of Dr. King's former professors of Christian ethics, Kenneth Lee "Snuffy" Smith. I got to be a student of Professor Smith.

In that course, I learned in great depth about the clarity Martin Luther King was seeking and communicating. While civil rights is what he is known for, I learned in Professor Smith's remarkable course that social justice was the true focus of Dr. King's prophecy. Social justice during King's life involved a spectrum of varied concerns, from poverty, to environmental issues (the first Earth Day was 1970, just 2 years after his death), opposition to the Vietnam War, concern about labor, and civil rights. Tavis Smiley writes eloquently about how, especially in the last year of his life, Martin Luther King was pressured unmercifully by close colleagues to focus only on civil rights and avoid what they saw as other social justice distractions.[2] Dr. King, however, had a full-spectrum view that could not be broken down into isolated categories, boxes, or labels. He saw a larger pattern of social injustice.

Dr. King was and is a clarity filter for so many, including me. Black people were labeled and discriminated against, but it was part of a larger pattern of injustice in his view. Like Peter Drucker, described in Chapter 1, Martin Luther King Jr. was a full-spectrum thinker before digital tools were there to help him.

Current Human Clarity Filters

The columnist Thomas L. Friedman spoke at Institute for the Future's 50th anniversary gathering on the future of trust at the Computer History Museum on September 27, 2018. He talked about his approach to journalism in today's turbulent world:

> I try to think without a box, not just outside the box. What can explain more things in more ways in more places for more days?

Many people think within existing boxes. Some think across the boxes. Some use boxes as a temporary scaffolding for new ideas before they are better understood. But very few think without a box to visualize a full spectrum of possibility. The boxes that we put people in will open up as our full-spectrum toolkit grows and our skills at full-spectrum thinking improve.

Friedman's current business card for *The New York Times* reads "Humiliation, Dignity, Trust, Leadership, Ownership & Amplification Columnist." These are words that provoke without-a-box conversations as he meets new people. Friedman helps readers understand current events and emerging future forces without forcing the conversation into a box. What I love about Tom Friedman's writing is that he jump-starts our ability to do full-spectrum thinking without telling us how to think or what to think.

Another example of a present-day human clarity filter is Ira Flatow's *Science Friday* program on public radio. On a Friday morning as I was writing this book, I heard him interview Mark Miodownik, the author of a book called *Liquid Rules: The Delightful and Dangerous Substances That Flow Through Our Lives.*

Liquids are all around us, but I realized as I listened to the show that I had a narrow category in my mind that I called "liquids." In fact, liquids are a spectrum—actually spectrums—of fluid possibilities. I didn't realize, for example, that peanut butter is a liquid and that you cannot carry it on an airplane. I didn't know that liquid soap is a really questionable product concept, since most of the soap is wasted and flows down the drain with an excess of water. Liquids are much more than they seem. I now think of liquids as a spectrum of possibilities. Under a full-spectrum lens, the daily life of liquids looks a lot different.

Science Friday is a provocative example of how to teach full-spectrum thinking to large groups of people. Here's how they describe their mission:

> For 25 years we've introduced top scientists to public radio listeners and reminded them how much fun it is to learn something new. But we're more than just a radio show. We produce award-winning digital videos, original web articles, and educational resources for teachers and informal educators. We like to say we're brain fun, for curious people.[3]

I'm sure everyone reading this book has a favorite author, columnist, podcast, or some other sense-making guide that provides a filter that you trust. In the future, we will still have trusted humans like Tom Friedman and Ira Flatow, but we will also have technology tools and media that will become much more powerful clarity filters for us. But each of us also has our own biases and blinders to consider. Clarity filters can challenge your assumptions, or they can channel you to see only things that you already believe.

In a scrambled future, where will we find clarity? How will we avoid misplaced certainty and false categorization? How can we moderate our certainty but develop our clarity? How can new digital tools help us do clarity filtering better?

Emergent Digital Clarity Filters

I am a futurist, not a technologist.[4] I think in future tense. I'm looking for big waves of change that are about to take off. I've learned through long experience in forecasting that most really big change takes 30 to 50 years to be an overnight success. Almost nothing that happens is truly new. Almost everything that happens was tried and failed years before—especially in the technology space. The question to ask is not, What's new? because if it is truly new, it is almost certainly not going to happen over the next decade. The question to ask is, What's ready to take off? and that is the focus of this chapter.

Over the next decade, a new wave of digital clarity filters will emerge to deal with the tangle of toxic misinformation and false certainty. People will need trustworthy ways of making sense out of what's going on around them—even when it doesn't make much sense at all. Clarity filters will give people powerful resources to reduce distrust and maybe even increase trust. Clarity filters will help us distinguish between clarity and certainty. Here are some key differences:

- Clarity is expressed in stories (Martin Luther King was a wonderful storyteller). Certainty is expressed in rules.

- Clarity includes curiosity about other points of view (Dr. King was curious about all aspects of social justice). Certainty has little curiosity.

- Clarity includes knowing what you don't know (Dr. King was both strong and humble). Certainty does not know what it doesn't know—and doesn't care to learn.

The new clarity filters won't be completely new. Rather, they will be aggregations of technologies and tools that have been tried in a variety of ways before. What will be new is increasing computing power, decreasing cost, and increasing ease of use by nontechnical people.

The new clarity filters will expand the range of options for both good and evil. I'm optimistic that people will use these new tools in much better ways. People need to focus on how to use the new tools in creative ways for good. Technology isn't inherently good or evil.

I met Kai-Fu Lee when he was the young technology genius at the right hand of John Sculley, who was then the CEO of Apple. Now Lee is a leading global expert on the future of artificial intelligence. In his book on the future of AI, he reflects on the deeper truth he has realized and that I now share:

> When it comes to understanding our AI future, we're all like those kindergartners. We're all full of questions without answers, trying to peer into the future with a mixture of childlike wonder and grown-up worries.[5]

In my 1988 book called *Groupware*,[6] I identified 17 approaches to group work through computers that signaled how computers could support teams, including group decision support, project management, presentation creation, text-filtering software, conversational structuring, group authoring, and nonhuman participants in team meetings. Nobody talks about "groupware" anymore, because computer support for business teams has become part of the fabric and process of working together. The term *groupware* played a temporary role in scoping out an emerging need and a set of tools that could help meet that need.

Now in 2020, we are seeing early signals, that I am calling clarity filters, that will follow a pattern similar to that of the signals of groupware in 1988. The term *clarity filters* might not stick, just as *groupware* didn't stick. But in the scrambled present and future, there is a growing need for clarity filters and a growing availability of emerging tools that will help.

The start-up called SoapAI that I opened this chapter with draws from an extremely wide range of sources across the story lines and echo chambers of broadcast news, political dogma, scientific inquiry, and social media conversations. Using AI and machine learning, SoapAI scours verified sources for anyone and everyone who is saying anything about everything. The challenge is how to verify and who will do the verification by what criteria. Could that process be hackable?

Machine learning makes the SoapAI scale of reach staggering. Big data analytics and visualization will empower sense-making in unimagined new ways. Gameful engagement makes it very easy to use.

Within SoapAI, the personalized overview of the most talked about topics and issues is presented through a graceful interface of bubbles, rather than lists. The bubbles can be sorted and rearranged on the screen to create new clusters based on the interests, values, and priorities of the user.

SoapAI software is in constant search of patterns in the news, and it explicitly challenges and looks beyond conventional categories. It seeks out new connections and new ways of thinking across a spectrum of possibilities.

SoapAI is one of the first in a new generation of clarity filters that I expect to grow rapidly. They are focusing on young people and how they can better make sense out of the news. With traditional media, many people used trusted editorial voices to help them make sense out of what was going on. Now, in the age of toxic misinformation, it is hard to know who to trust. Distrust is rampant.

SoapAI prequalifies thousands of sources such as scientists, executives, politicians, and celebrities on the most-talked-about issues and ideas. Information is clustered into bubbles that help users "clean" the complex sources in their own personal quest for clarity. By creating a spectrum of perspectives, users are able to see patterns and form educated opinions with the knowledge that they are engaging with a variety of perspectives that have been verified by explicit criteria.

SoapAI helps users refine their own points of view by using the value of multiple—and sometimes contrasting—sources. It provides varied context to fuel contextual thinking. It provides perspective beyond the day-to-day hour-by-hour frenzy of news that dominates the cable channels. SoapAI is focused on seeking and surfacing trusted sources, relieving overload, and cleaning (hence the bubbles) its vast database of multiple sources. It is like a smart analyst who never sleeps. While most of today's social media scour for fake news after it is already out there, SoapAI does filtering of prequalified sources before accepting inputs.

Clarity filters like SoapAI will help users develop a full-spectrum view. They will nudge you down a path of contextual thinking around bubbles of conversation, topics, and stories.

The Neuroscience of Clarity vs. Certainty

Clarity is the ability to see through messes and contradictions to a future that others cannot yet see. Leaders will need to be very clear about where they are going, but very flexible about how they get there.[7] In the scrambled present, there are many dilemmas—problems that can't be solved and won't go away, but we have to try to make sense out of them and act anyway, even with incomplete information and only partial visibility. The leadership skill I call "dilemma flipping" is a discipline that thrives in the space between deciding too soon (the classic mistake of the problem solver or the true believer) and deciding too late (the classic mistake of the academic).[8] Leaders must be a source of clarity, and people will yearn for clarity in the scrambled future ahead.

There is a big difference between clarity and certainty. The neurologist Robert Burton explored how our brains long for certainty and often fool us:

> Despite how certainty feels, it is neither a conscious choice nor even a thought process. Certainty and similar states of "knowing we know" arise out of involuntary brain mechanisms that, like love and anger, function independently of reason.[9]

We are gaining a neurological understanding of the differences between clarity and certainty. Burton's remarkable work reminds me of the social science concept of confirmation bias, which essentially is the idea that continuing with existing beliefs is easier than adopting new ones. It is easier to believe that new experiences conform to things you already think you know, rather than to imagine them as something new or different than you have experienced. Modern cognitive science and neuroscience use the concept of "myside bias" to describe how people can fall into believing things—even if they are not true—as long as others in our social networks believe that those things are true.

Many people are certain, but few are clear. Categorization is a form of certainty when the categories go unchallenged. The opposite of clarity is not confusion, it is certainty.

Clarity is fuzzy around the edges. My colleague Jamais Cascio thinks of clarity as "good enough" thinking for your own purposes without the need to keep pursuing precision—or perhaps precision is not even possible. Clarity is fuzzier than certainty and that's OK.

New digital clarity filters will reduce the fuzziness and they are almost here. Toxic misinformation will require powerful filters, and—just in time—those filters are starting to appear even today. New technology and media tools will enable and amplify much more robust forms of full-spectrum thinking to help make sense out of the future in order to draw out insights and make better decisions in the present.

Today's tools often force us into categories we did not choose. Marketing and advertising segments us in ways that allow companies to sell to us more easily. Social media draw us into interest groups that categorize and filter for us. Today's media make it easy to hear from only those people with whom you already agree. The underlying technology of binary computing means that, ultimately, everything must be reduced to a zero or a one. Binary choices, however, will yield to spectrums of choice.

The Capabilities of Digital Clarity Filters

The emerging tools will help us make sense out of the scramble all around us. The emerging clarity filters will help us think across gradients of possibility and avoid premature categorization by creative use of

- Ubiquitous sensing

- Pattern visualization

- Gameful engagement

- Sense-making aids

In a world where ubiquitous cheap sensors are everywhere, our bodies and the medications we use will be always-on. Whereas health care now functions "outside in," as we are observed, poked, and prodded by the humans and machines we call care providers, 10 years from now our "health care" (more just sick care today) will come from inside our bodies and move out. In diabetes care, we are already seeing hints of this potential.

The visualization of all that sensor data will help us to see the hidden patterns in healthy living and to make better decisions. Big data is worthless unless we have the analytics to understand what's going on. Innovation in big data has focused on computational capability for massive data collection. Now, organizations are collecting more data than they will ever use. That same data is at risk of being hacked and misused, undermining trust in the entire process and the companies involved.

Visualization will allow us to step inside complex data sets, rather than rely on statistics and normal curves to generalize and derive meaning from data in second- or thirdhand ways. We will be able to understand with our bodies, not just with our minds. Computing in the future will be an immersive and ambient learning environment for humans. It will eventually include haptics: the ability to touch and feel the data around us. Today's virtual reality video games come the closest today to this kind of experience, and the kids are experiencing it before the adults.

What we currently call video gaming and storytelling will evolve into media for emotionally laden attention in a wide variety of forms that ultimately will help us make better sense out of the world around us. (More on this in Chapter 9.) Neuroscience will help us understand how our brains function and categorize our experiences. Neuroscience will get practical over the next decade, and it will help us learn and practice clarity filtering.

This won't be pure technology innovation, but rather a creative mix of technology, connectivity, and new human skills that will come most easily to digital natives. (More on this in Chapter 6.) This blending will create a potent variety of ways for people to navigate misinformation, disinformation, and weaponized categorization of others.

I am not suggesting that clarity vs. certainty is a binary choice or an easy choice. In search of clarity, we will encounter many of the same cognitive biases that are imbedded in unexamined certainty. For example, will the ubiquitous cheap sensors be measuring the right things? What are the sensors missing? Are we forcing data into visualizations that hide as much truth as they reveal? Are we creating playful narratives that are not revealing stories that help us learn? And finally, what happens when an issue truly *doesn't* make sense? In a scrambled future, many things just won't make sense even with the best clarity filters. Clarity filters need to be designed and used in such a way that they avoid the illusion of objectivity when there is none present. What will clarity about the nonsensical look like?

The stakes are up and they will go up even more in the future. In early 2019, the Munich Security Conference was organized around the theme ·NATO at 70: An Alliance in Crisis. At the conference, Brad Smith, president and chief legal officer of Microsoft, warned that "AI is everything," a game changer like electricity. He described the present as a "Sputnik moment" and said, "This is the hardest tech challenge the US has ever faced."[10] Both China and Russia are challenging the US, and they are just the obvious competitors. Loosely structured terrorist groups may be an even bigger risk. Brad Smith used the term *AI* (for "artificial intelligence") expansively to include machine learning, where computers learn on their own. We see strong hints of that already. AI has huge potential, in collaboration with human thinking, to open up new ways of understanding the interconnectedness of what may appear to be discrete. The early applications, however, will be driven by profit and the desire to control.

The Analytics of Clarity Filters

On June 7, 2018, I brought a group of executives to the corporate headquarters of Electronic Arts (EA) in Redwood Shores, California. EA is one of the world's most successful video game publishing companies. We met with Zach Anderson, chief analytics officer at EA. He shared with us how EA can track (anonymously) all of the detailed moves of every player in a game. Using advanced analytics and visualization, combined with fluid gaming interfaces, Anderson's team at EA is able to understand the patterns of player behavior with great depth. He said it this way:

I like distributions, not lines. I don't like to normalize.
Now, we can look at full distributions and see the patterns.[11]

Just in time, because the three external future forces I outlined in Chapter 3 will *require* leaders to do spectrum thinking. With big data analytics and the ability to visualize data spatially, leaders will be able to *see* the spectrum from the inside and *do* spectrum thinking. Most importantly, leaders will be able to see new patterns and seek new clarity.

Normal curves and statistics are limited tools that invite us to force fit complex new experiences into standardized categories. Like other forms of categorical thinking, they are powerful but require disciplined use. New technology and media tools will make it possible to literally go *inside* a large distribution of numbers, rather than merely categorizing or summarizing what might be going on. As a person who never liked statistics anyway, I am relieved and hopeful about this transition. Who needs statistics if you can go inside a distribution and see patterns directly? This will be an important new form of full-spectrum thinking. EA and others are showing us how it is taking shape now.

In March of 2019, 800 scientists signed a manifesto in *Nature* calling on people to stop using the categorical system called statistical significance. Their biggest argument: "Statistically significant" or "not statistically significant" is too often misinterpreted to mean either "the study worked" or "the study did not work." A "true" effect can sometimes yield a statistical test result of greater than the established threshold of truth. And we know from recent years that science is rife with false-positive studies that achieved values of less than the usual threshold. The *Nature* authors argue that math is not the problem. Instead, it's human psychology. Bucketing results into "statistically significant" and "statistically non-significant," they write, leads to a too black-and-white approach to scrutinizing science.[12]

I doubt that this change in science will come easily, but this is a clear call for full-spectrum thinking about research results by scientists who know the limits of the system they are using.

These emerging tools will make it possible to create more positive futures because leaders will be able to see the full spectrum of possibilities before they decide what to do. Such advanced foresight will help leaders draw out both new insight and better-informed action. Leaders will be able to make better decisions in the present.

Full-spectrum thinking will also help people avoid the nasty traps of categorical thinking. The present is already too complicated for many people, and it's going to get worse. People will yearn desperately for simple explanations. Simple is fine, but simplistic will be dangerous. Comforting categories from the past might seem like a relief, but they will come at a cost and with great risk. Categorize with caution. Consider a full spectrum of possibilities first. Be careful who and what you trust.

Clarity Filtering for Trust

Clarity-filtered stories will need to be trusted in order to have value. My IFTF colleague Jane McGonigal is teaching at the intersection of futures thinking and neuroscience. Here's how she summarizes one of her core lessons:

> We usually think of trust and distrust as direct opposites. But in the brain, trust and distrust are two entirely separate systems. They are not opposite ends of the same continuum.[13]

Trust is rational, hard to build, fragile, and created through direct experience. Trust is difficult to seed through use of social and broadcast media. Distrust, on the other hand, is emotional, easy to build, and resilient. Distrust can come from rumor and secondhand information. It is easy to seed distrust through social media. We think of trust and distrust as being on a single spectrum, but they actually arise from two different patterns of connection in our brains.

Each year, Institute for the Future chooses a focus for its foundational forecasting efforts, and in 2018 IFTF chose to focus on trust, distrust, and mistrust. As part of this research, IFTF identified four core models of trust—all of which help us imagine how clarity filters will be designed to seed trust and hedge against distrust:

Trust through continuous verification: striving for certainty in a world of infinite data. While certainty is impossible, we strive for it anyway. Clarity is achievable and the emerging tools will help us reach that goal.

Trust by boundary protection: building digital fences in a world without borders. Both fences and bridges will be possible, but both will be fragile.

Trust by outsourced authority: relying on experts in a world of confusion. In our experience at IFTF, expertise rarely correlates with celebrity. For our opinion aggregation forecasts, we seek out experts at forecasting the future who either are not yet or don't want to be celebrities.

Trust by protective filtering: designing custom views in a world of infinite realities. Filters will be mandatory, but they must embody trust.

Clarity filters will need to incorporate at least one of these models of trust in order to be viable. Ideally, clarity filters should address the trust challenges of each of these models. Trust is elusive, distrust is everywhere, and mistrust will be the norm. Scrambling with distrust will be an everyday activity, but there will be lots of digital filtering to help people offset the digital distortions.

In this chapter, we have introduced the growing importance of clarity filters, both human (like Tom Friedman and Ira Flatow) and digitally assisted (like SoapAI and EA's use of analytics), to help us make sense of the present scramble—which is getting increasingly scrambled. Ubiquitous sensors, visualization, gaming, and a growing range of sense-making aids are becoming practical already. The key will be to grow trusted sources that allow us to make sense out of the external world.

The new clarity filters won't provide complete full-spectrum thinking, but they will at least encourage broad-spectrum thinking—beyond the boxes and categories of the past. We are moving toward full-spectrum thinking even though we may never fully get there. Clarity filters won't be perfect, but they will be much better than what we have relied on in the past. Chapter 5 will explore the networks that will connect the tools of the present in ways that will involve both more connectivity and more distributed authority.

CHAPTER 5

Distributed-Authority Networks

Scrambling for Control

DISTRIBUTED-AUTHORITY NETWORKS, JUST BEGINNING TO play out in our world today, actually got their start more than 50 years ago. I think of the history of the internet to date as the world's largest market test for what will happen next.

Up to now, common sense would tell us that control implies central authority—but that is not the world that is emerging. Central authority and clearly defined categories of control are breaking down into a much more distributed world that will be linked together through digital connectivity. We are on that path already in 2020, but this is just the beginning.

A new kind of connectivity is taking shape today as we move from centralized to decentralized to truly distributed networks. In the world of computer networks, authority has been centralized in categories of power that embody and enforce trust—like banks. In today's world, banks don't always look so trustworthy anymore. Distrust abounds. Gradually, networks of computers are creating new ways to distribute trust.

Rigid centralized categories are giving way to distributed fluid categories across multiple spectrums. Central comput*ers* (*separate* machines) are giving way to distributed comput*ing* (*connected* machines). In order to understand what's next, we need to look back even as we look forward.

I had just finished my PhD and was teaching in a sociology department at a small liberal arts college when my first professional paper was accepted by the International Conference on Computer Communications for the conference called ICCC '72. I had only applied because I had misunderstood the title of the conference.

My paper, coauthored with computer scientist Jim Schuyler, who I had met when we were both graduate students at Northwestern, focused on people communicating with people through computer networks. ICCC '72 was actually supposed to be about computers communicating with other computers.

Because of my lucky misunderstanding, on October 24, 1972, I ended up at what turned out to be a historic gathering at the Washington Hilton Hotel in Washington, DC, where what we know as "the internet" today was introduced publicly. The unofficial purpose of the conference was to introduce this new computer network that had limited initial goals at the time but would eventually change the world. The ARPANET, as it was called then, was intended for data communication among computers at defense contractor universities.

Fortunately for me and Jim, there were a few others with similar interests in people communicating with people through computers, and the organizers put us all in the same session:

- Douglas C. Engelbart, the father of the mouse, hypermedia, and so much more.

- Murray Turoff, the developer of the first online systems for emergency preparedness in the federal government.

- Andrew Lipinski from Institute for the Future, which had an ARPA[1] contract to develop an online Delphi network, as well as an NSF[2] grant to study how it could be used for aggregating expert opinion.

- Jim Schuyler and me, presenting our research involving online questionnaires. Jim and I were the youngest and the least known of the panelists.

All the other speakers were far more advanced in their thinking than I was, and that conference turned out to be another turning point in my life.

At the end of our panel of people-oriented presenters, a passionate young man in the back of the room lost his patience and confronted us with the fact that we never should have been allowed into this conference in the first place. He stood up and shouted something like this, his voice cracking with anger as he yelled: "The use of the ARPANET for people communicating with people is a misuse of CPU!" Then he stormed out of the room.

I sometimes wonder what became of that young man, but I must admit that his judgment about our misfit panel was correct at the time. We were definitely suggesting that the ARPANET be used for things it was not intended to do. Time has shown that the uses we were exploring on that panel were even more important than the original purpose.

The Long Journey toward Distributed-Authority Networks

When I later joined Institute for the Future, I learned that packet switching, the core technology of the ARPANET, was designed by Paul Baran and others to resist nuclear attack. The new network was intended to protect the United States from its enemy the USSR. The effort got started in 1964, amid the Cold War.[3] Networks in those days were dangerously centralized and vulnerable to attack from the other superpowers. Packet switching allowed signals to be broken down into "packets" when they were sent and not reassembled until they reached their destination. Centralized networks were dangerous because they were all in one place. Distributed networks were much more spread out and thus safer. Resources were harder to find and harder to attack. The side effect was that the emerging organizational structure had no center, grew from the edges, and was much harder to control. Ironically, this same distributed network is now being used by the Russians for disinformation attacks on US elections.

Paul Baran was one of the founders of Institute for the Future, and I got to know him after I came to Silicon Valley in 1973. I learned later that his original name for packet switching was "hot potato routing." That original name reflects much more accurately where I think we are going in the near future.

The distributed authority made possible by hot potato routing is starting

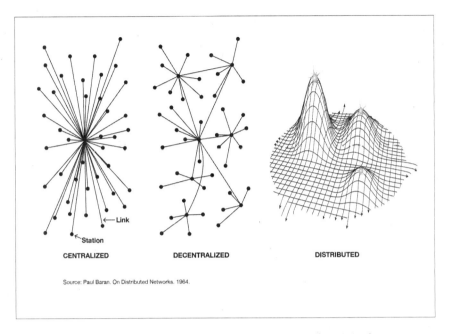

CENTRALIZED   DECENTRALIZED   DISTRIBUTED

Source: Paul Baran. On Distributed Networks. 1964.

FIGURE 5.1: The left two graphics are from Paul Baran's original 1964 paper describing the concept of what came to be called "packet switching" to create truly distributed, not just decentralized, computing. The vision of distributed computing is very consistent with what I call "shape-shifting" organizations today.

to scale. Distributed-authority computing will become practical on a global scale. Figure 5.1 shows the shift from centralized to decentralized to distributed, in graphic summary, that first appeared in 1964 but is now poised to have much broader impacts. The sources of trust will become more distributed and more embodied in computer networks. The greatest power will be at the edges, not the center.

Today's global corporations started to become more distributed long ago. I did my first project with P&G just a few years after the ARPANET was introduced at the Washington Hilton. I was studying the net (before it became the web) through NSF and ARPA grants to Institute for the Future. P&G came to us and asked how they could learn about the net and explore how it might contribute to their research and development efforts around the world. They created, with IFTF's input, a prototype system they called ION, which provided something very much like what we call social media today, for their R&D scientists around the world. It scaled very quickly, and they had 35,000 users before P&G had an official e-mail system.

P&G had always believed in the value of communication among their scientists (what was called at the time the "invisible college" of scientists), but most of that communication happened through informal in-person meetings, more-formal letters, and very formal journal papers. And, the conversation in those days was rigidly proprietary to P&G.

When e-mail became more popular and the ARPANET gradually evolved into a more public internet, I remember the controversy over whether new P&G scientists could put their e-mail addresses on their business cards. This was a particular problem for new P&G graduates, who were used to invisible colleges of scientists that were much more open than the closed P&G world allowed. A new spectrum of communication options was starting to crack open.

In 1973, Jacques Vallée and I facilitated what might have been the first international social media exchange through what we now call the internet. I heard recently from one of the participants, psychologist Ederyn Williams, who was then at the Communications Studies Group at University College London. Ederyn revealed himself as perhaps the first anonymous (and very polite) troll called The Sons of the Soil. This form of group text communication was just becoming possible, and the subject of our conversation was which medium is good for what. It was already becoming clear in 1973 that there would be a spectrum of media options, including in-person meetings. This was part of the evolution from computer networking to social networking through computers.

The Geopolitical Risk of Distributed Authority

When I was guest lecturing recently for new three-star generals at the Army War College, I was on the program right before Madeleine Albright, whose latest book is called *Fascism: A Warning*.[4] She grew up in Eastern Europe and experienced fascism firsthand in her family. The challenge she raises is whether, in organizations that are increasingly shape-shifting, we lose the ability to govern ourselves and it becomes easier for authoritarianism to gain traction as a simplistic relief from complex problems and pain.

Robert O. Work, the former deputy secretary of defense under President

Obama, expressed a similar concern at the Munich Security Conference in 2019:

> AI gives tyranny new tools it never had before and makes it more powerful than it has ever been before. We are entering a period of intense technological challenge.

In the next war, he predicted, it will be "our AI against their AI, and the side with the best AI wins."[5]

While I have great respect for both Albright and Work, I am much less worried about authoritarianism than either of them. In a world where anything that can be distributed will be distributed, I believe it will be harder for fascism or authoritarianism to scale. Certainly, this kind of central-control thinking can work for a while, but I doubt it can scale or sustain itself. The media for distributed dissent will be too powerful, I believe, to be controlled.

I understand that there is a counterargument. Big centralized companies can acquire smaller companies that are distributed. Countries like Singapore or China can attempt to control networks and keep them centralized. While efforts like this are real and can certainly slow down the shift toward distributed networks, the debate in my mind is not about whether but about when distributed-authority networks will scale.

On the other hand, shape-shifting organizational structures may become so limp that they lose a common sense of direction and purpose. As the author Michelle Dean said so eloquently: "Authority has become something diffuse and flammable, like spray paint."[6]

Distributed-authority computing is here today in limited ways. For example, Institute for the Future began studying blockchain in 2014, and as we mapped the growing variety of activities and ideas, we developed this definition and tested it over a period of years:

> Blockchain is distributed computing that can
> track the status of autonomous virtual objects and
> provide security *without central authority.*

Blockchain, an early example of distributed networks, builds on the internet to create a platform that moves away from rigid central categories toward fluid distribution of trust and control. Blockchain infrastructure promises a new way of organizing ourselves in a global society. Blockchain does categorize in more certain ways with multiple points of authority that the user chooses. Blockchain creates a locked-in version of the truth that cannot be manipulated. It is a consistent shared record of the truth according to the transaction record—not according to any central authority. You can think of blockchain as distributed trust.

Blockchain has the potential to provide high-trust interaction in low-trust environments, although the case is still out and it may fail in the long run. Even if it does fail, however, it is bound to fail in an interesting way that will yield important lessons. Users can build trust by collecting multiple instances of people trusting them. But blockchains are just a start, and blockchain is now where the internet was in the early 1990s. Distributed authority will be amplified by new forms of distributed computing such as blockchain. Think of blockchain today as a family of prototypes for the future. Blockchain is a directional hint of where distributed-authority computing will be moving.

In 2017, IFTF's Blockchain Futures Lab did a 10-year forecast (2017–2027) that focused on how blockchain will reshape the world at the intersection of money, technology, and human identity:

> Over the coming decade, audacious blockchain experiments will reshape the way we think about everything from cash to computing, from identity to governance. Starting from today's cryptocurrencies, these experiments will build on the unique affordances of blockchain architectures to create radical zones of transformation. They will catalyze—and be catalyzed by—advances in artificial intelligence, virtual reality, and the Internet of Things. These chain reactions will coalesce to create a global infrastructure for trusted computing that will touch every sector, every market, every household.[7]

Trust in a World of Distributed Authority

The phrase *trusted computing* is up for renegotiation. Traditionally, trust in computing networks came from some sort of central authority, like a bank or a company that operated the computer or the network. The promise of blockchain is high-trust interaction in low-trust environments. Blockchain provides a distributed unchangeable ledger or log of information—with no central authority in charge. I've been studying blockchain for more than five years now, and I still get a headache when I think about it.

Blockchain is mind stretching, since it moves beyond categories with which we are comfortable. Rather than fixed central authority, blockchain is fluid distributed authority. Rather than centralized trust, blockchain promises distributed trust. The categories of trust are fluid and distributed—not centralized. The case on blockchain is still out, however.

Vitalik Buterin, the founder of the Ethereum blockchain, puts it this way when he talks about the implications of distributing authority:

> Whereas most technologies tend to automate workers on the periphery doing menial tasks, blockchains automate away at the center. Instead of putting the taxi driver out of a job, blockchain puts Uber out of a job and lets the driver work with the customer directly.[8]

It is important to note that a reputable rider will still need some way to find a qualified driver. Blockchain distributes authority, but it still requires trust. Can an algorithm deliver a trusted service without a human corporation in the middle?

Blockchain also raises the question of what a human-led organization can offer that an algorithm cannot. I believe that there will continue to be good answers to that question, but many companies today don't have one.

Trust is embodied in categories that today's computers force us into. Ultimately, they force us into zeros and ones. Today's computers want to finish our sentences and autocorrect our mistakes.

Digital computers use categories instead of continuous measurement. They contain comparisons, "if" statements, procedures, and arithmetic. Computers as we know them today are relentless binary categorization machines, even if they have a touch of fuzzy logic.

But distributed-authority computing is scaling fast, and quantum computing is on the horizon. The move from centralized to decentralized to distributed began a long time ago, but it will take off over the next decade. Blockchain-based services are probing whether or not distributed-authority networks are truly ready to scale. Distributed-authority computing—especially quantum computing—is introducing a new paradigm like those described by Thomas Kuhn in his *Structure of Scientific Revolutions* that I introduced in Chapter 2.

New forms of computing will enable us to create systems that don't rely on static categories. Right now, our computing systems implicitly encourage us to use rigid categories whether we like it or not. Doug Merritt, the CEO of the data analytics company called Splunk, said it this way at a meeting of Silicon Valley CEOs where I was speaking recently: "IT systems designed to order the disorderly VUCA world are dangerous. There are a limited number of systems designed to operate within chaos—to find the patterns and benefits within disorder."[9]

Blending Human and Machine

It is clear to me that distributed-authority computing will require a blend of human and computing resources. The blending was prototyped recently in the experience of AlphaGo, the deep neural network program developed in the UK by DeepMind (since acquired by Google) on a team led by Demis Hassabis. The stated goal of DeepMind is to "fundamentally understand intelligence," which I take to mean both machine and human intelligence.

I believe that the key challenge of distributed-authority computing over the next decade will be how to distribute tasks between humans and computing. What will humans do best? What will computing do best?

The documentary *AlphaGo* is a poignant human-computer love story. In the end, the AlphaGo program defeated legendary Go player Lee Sedol, but in defeat the human player found a new dimension of himself. The defeat disrupted the way Go is played.

Go is the most complex game ever devised by humans, the oldest continuously played board game, and the holy grail of AI challenges. Go is a spectrum-thinking game with fluid categories and playing field. In ancient China, playing Go was one of four noble accomplishments of learning, along with music, poetry, and painting. AlphaGo is a machine that learns on its own and stretches the limits of binary computing.

AlphaGo defeated Lee Sedol four games to one in the match and showed creativity on a different spectrum than that of the human player. Lee

Sedol was defeated but felt his humanness was expanded after playing this inanimate being.

One of the analysts after the match observed: "This experience will influence how Go is played for the next thousand years." When a computer defeated a legendary human Go player, it wasn't the end of the Go game—it was the beginning of new ways to play Go.

Sales of Go games increased after the match, and Lee Sedol claims that playing AlphaGo has improved his game. "This experience made me grow. I intend to use the lessons I have learned. I am grateful and I think, I think I found my reason to play Go. I realize that it was really a good choice to play Go. It is an unforgettable experience."[10] This is a player who seemed arrogant before playing but who gained a new humility.

Neural networks and machine learning make it possible to visualize full-spectrum complexity—even the complexity of Go. Distributed-authority computing makes it possible to distribute skills across a wild new mix of human and computing resources.

Augmented Intelligence, Not Artificial Intelligence

The first workshop I did around *The New Leadership Literacies* was for a group of chief human resources officers organized by LinkedIn and held at CSAIL,[11] the lab at MIT where the term *artificial intelligence* was coined. We were told at the meeting that the term was 65 years old when we held our meeting in the summer of 2017. There had been a debate, at the time it was named, over whether to call it "artificial intelligence" or "augmented intelligence." Unfortunately, *artificial* intelligence won.

Augmented intelligence was the term favored by Douglas C. Engelbart, the most prominent member of the panel at ICCC '72 that I mentioned earlier. Engelbart founded and led the Augmentation Research Center (ARC) at what was then Stanford Research Institute (now SRI International), which was the first library and resource center for the ARPANET. The prototype system that he created was called NLS (roughly translated as "online system," as I recall), which was a powerful mix of capabilities that Engelbart imagined would address the world's most complex problems. He had been inspired by Vannevar Bush and his classic 1945 concept of the Memex,[12] a world brain.

Engelbart's expectation was that building a machine that would help solve the world's problems would be very complicated indeed. He once said that the number of commands in NLS would equal the number of words in the English language. The power of categories comes when you have a wide range of expressions embodied in commands and concepts, with operations to bring them to life. Engelbart built a very complex system to address very complex problems. He took categorization to a whole new level. He used computers to help people think differently.

Steve Jobs had quite another vision of computers that began with ease of use. He wanted to minimize the number of commands and make computers as intuitive as possible. Eventually, Jobs would help computers evolve into digital appliances. Jobs admired Engelbart's work but longed to simplify it—which led to a basic tension between Jobs and Engelbart.[13]

Engelbart was creating a mountain bike, he said, while he saw Jobs creating a tricycle. You can ride a tricycle right away, but you can't do much with it. A mountain bike is hard to ride in difficult terrain but much more powerful once you get skilled in using it.

With distributed-authority computing, we will have the potential of mountain bike performance with tricycle ease of use. Both Engelbart and Jobs imagined such power, but the computing and the networks weren't ready yet. Today, companies like DeepMind and experiments like AlphaGo are drawing from the visions of Engelbart and Jobs to combine power with ease of use.

Distributed-authority networks still require human intervention at key points in the trust cycle. There is a looming fear that computers will do exactly what we ask them to do, but in a really awful way. Humans have the context to make judgments about unexpected and unintended consequences, even when we cannot create precise instructions. Computers do not have that context.

When the internet was first imagined in the late 1960s, there was one Cold War enemy: the centralized and bureaucratic USSR. Today, the military is scrambling to control terrorist networks—some of which are led by nation-states, but others are not. The increasingly distributed networks will need to constrain the increasingly distributed forces of terror and disruption in the future. And the military is not alone in facing asymmetric competition.

Newspapers are scrambling for control in a world where citizen journalists are everywhere and everyone has a camera in their phone. People are scrambling for control in a world with fewer jobs but more ways to make a living. The scramble feels overwhelming to many people.

It has been a long journey toward distributed-authority computing, but in a real sense, that journey is just beginning to get interesting. Over the next decade, distributed-authority computing will scale. The politics of distributed-authority computing will get increasingly volatile, and trust will be a looming issue.

What this technological shift toward distributed-authority networks means for individuals is that people can be connected and work globally through digital networks. What it means for organizations is that hierarchies won't work nearly as well as they used to work. The media for full-spectrum thinking and full-spectrum connectivity are set to explode over the next decade. Categorizing or labeling scientists as inside or outside any company is increasingly difficult. Also, the balance between more-open exchanges and proprietary information will shift toward more-open. What it means for societies is that we are interconnected and thus interdependent whether we like it or not. Anything that can be distributed will be distributed.

Fortunately, the young leaders are entering the adult world with a big competitive advantage that will surprise many in their parents' generation. These young people will guide the clarity filters and distributed networks of the future. I'm optimistic about their abilities to do just that.

CHAPTER 6

The True
Digital Natives

Scrambling with the Social Order

TEN YEARS FROM NOW, WHAT WE CALL "VIDEO GAMING" today will be viewed as the most powerful learning medium in history. And the kids are already ahead of us in learning how to use this new medium.

In the movie *Ender's Game*, a top military leader (played by Harrison Ford) explains to a young prodigy named Ender: "We need minds like yours: young people integrate complex data more easily than adults." In the Orson Scott Card novel and the movie, young people were trained to be warriors through immersive video gaming experiences.[1]

As I am completing this book, the video game called Fortnite is very popular with kids and very worrisome for many parents. Fortnite, developed by Epic Games as a clever variation on an earlier less successful game they had done, creates a safe virtual space for kids to gather for unstructured play time. They team up and play through fresh stories and new adventures. The developers keep feeding in new ways to interact and play through the environment. In the summer of 2019, Anthony Palumbi published an insightful opinion piece in *The Washington Post* entitled "Hey Parents, Stop Worrying and Learn to Love 'Fortnite,'" with this conclusion:

If you're a parent inclined to limit screen time, it's worth taking a deep breath. Rather than treating games such as "Fortnite" as the enemy, make time to ask your kid to show you what they're building there. Ask about the friends they've made and the skills they've learned.[2]

Many parents view today's video games as threats they need to manage. Instead of learning about the world of video gaming with their kids, many parents just try to limit play with crude constraints like "screen time." Video game use is indeed a big parenting challenge (I believe many of today's games are too sexual and too violent), but it is also an unprecedented opportunity for cross-generational learning. The medium of gaming will be far more important than today's content.

A youthquake of true digital natives will enter the workforce over the next decade with a competitive advantage based largely on their experience as gamers and native users of digital media. They know how to upskill themselves and organize into teams, because they learned how by playing video games.

The True Digital Natives

I have a very specific definition of *digital native*. I see digital natives as a threshold shift—not a generational cohort—that began in 2010 when the iPhone and the iPad introduced a new media ecology beyond the separate early digital tools that had preceded them. Figure 6.1 gives my timeline summary of the waves of change of the internet that created the true digital natives.

The Apple Newton (the first graceful digital appliance and tablet) was introduced in 1993. It was a business failure by 1998, but it failed in a very interesting way. Roughly a decade later, the iPhone and then the iPad built on the experience of the Newton. The new media ecology became possible and scalable.

Psychologists tell us that most kids start to become adults in their early teens, depending on the kid and the culture. The young people who started to become adults in 2010 or later are different from a neuroscience point of view, as well as psychologically and sociologically—but we don't know

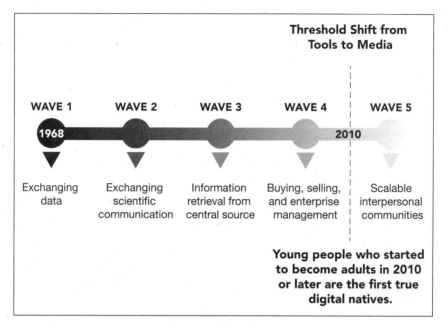

FIGURE 6.1: Timeline showing key stages in the development of the internet, highlighting the 2010 threshold where the digital native phenomenon began.

yet just *how* different they will be as adults. We do know that they are very difficult to categorize and that they don't like being categorized. We do know that the younger they are, the stronger the impact of digital media is.

There Is Great Positive Potential

While I view the introduction of the digital natives into the workforce as a wonderful but challenging cross-generational learning opportunity, many of my social science colleagues are focusing on the negatives and are quick to blame the kids, the internet, Apple, Google, Facebook, or something else. I certainly can understand—and often share—their concerns, but the impact of digital media is a really tough subject to study, and the results the way I see them are mixed, with positives and negatives. Labeling kids as depressed or dangerous because of digital media may have some truth to it, but it is a very unfortunate place to start an analysis. The true digital natives are more an opportunity than a threat.

In my PhD program at Northwestern, I learned how to do social science research on the impacts of technology. I was taught to look for a clean "independent variable" so you can study the impacts on dependent variables. "Screen time," for example, is not a clean independent variable, except in some limited neuroscience ways (for example, the finding that looking at screens before going to bed is not good for sleep). Otherwise, I just don't think "screen time" is a good variable to study in terms of long-term impact, although it is easy to measure. Ten years from now, anything could function as a screen. I'm much more concerned about what kids (and parents) are *doing* through the screen. Limiting screen time is just too simplistic, even though it is tempting for parents looking for something they can control.

Social scientists, in my experience, often are tempted by the easiest variables to measure. When studying the impacts of new digital media, unfortunately, there are no easy independent variables to study.

As a futurist trained as a social scientist, I'd like to see scholars, physicians, and pundits view digital media as opportunities for cross-generational learning as well as potential trouble. Instead, many voices of authority are just focusing on the problems and dilemmas (and I agree that there are many problems). Those of us who are not digital natives (and I include myself, although I had an identity on the internet's predecessor beginning in 1972) have a lot to learn from young people. We digital immigrants all need true digital native mentors. Certainly, we have something to offer as digital immigrants, but I believe we have a lot to learn from the true digital natives.

Kids are born with full-spectrum thinking, but adults, schools, and society often force it out of them with education, testing, technology, and culture. If adults use full-spectrum thinking to learn about the true digital natives, it will get much closer to reality.

Digital immigrants (all of us who are 25 or older in 2020) will have a chance to play the wisdom game across generations. Age does matter and, as we advance in age, we can learn to see things in a deeper way. Younger is not necessarily better, but neither is older. Traditional generational cohort analysis (think "Gen Z") will be too simplistic to understand the emerging age spectrum.

Below is a forecast of the true digital natives as we are coming to know them today. This profile draws from IFTF's forecast for the college student class of 2030 that we did recently for SNHU. We identified the most important future forces that will shape young people—looking 10 years ahead—and linked those to the emerging profile of the true digital natives and their behaviors today.

My Forecast for the True Digital Natives

These young people are beyond the 2010 threshold (see Figure 6.1), and they are the first wave of the true digital natives. They will be shaped by driving forces of the digital world, but they will also be able to use these media in ways that workers were never capable of doing before. These young people are already disrupting how we learn, how we work, and how we organize. They are learners, but they have their own ways of learning. They won't be sure about the value of a college degree or graduate degrees (the next decade will be a reckoning for the economic value of degrees), but they know they don't want the student loan debt that many students and parents are still burdened with today. Many have what researcher Linda Stone first called "continuous partial attention,"[3] which can have both positive and negative characteristics. At their best, they can do multiple things at once and still have a focus. Digital immigrants call this "multitasking." In contrast, usually the more tasks *we* do, the less well we do them. I think that the digital natives will be different in the following ways:

The true digital natives will excel at human-computer collaboration. Artificial intelligence, machine learning, and robotics are rapidly extending the role of smart machines into every facet of human endeavor. Human–machine collaborations are reinventing the way we learn, the way we create value, and the way we build the world around us.

Digital agents like virtual assistants, bots, and avatars act on our behalf, tapping into massive sets of data about every individual. Algorithms—the rules that define a process in computer code—make judgments, recommendations, and decisions about how we spend our time, money, knowledge, and social capital. Robots perform both conceptual and physical tasks, often in partnership with humans.

These young people have the ability to discover and participate in mixed human–machine learning communities, often distributed in worldwide networks. The concept of taking a class or course will transform into an emergent learning community and new ways to accredit those communities. Young people move strategically between managing and being managed by intelligent machines. Machine agents are becoming part of the learning process. Worker-learners need to both direct and be directed by these agents.

The true digital natives will have their own personal economies. As the unemployment rate for young people remains high worldwide and new work platforms reorganize work into a "gig economy" of consultants, freelancers, Uber-style workers, and internet celebrities, more and more people are building personal economies around their individual portfolios of skills, resources, and public identities. A critical goal of education is to prepare people of all ages for building these positive, sustainable personal economies. Milton Chen of Edutopia is calling for personalized "ed-*you*-cation" to prepare for this kind of world of work and learning. True digital natives are mastering the art of getting paid to learn, and educational institutions are shifting from fee-based learning providers to percentage-based learning brokers. The challenge is to flip the on-demand model of work to create one's own personal businesses or use existing platforms to market one's personal skills and knowledge to targeted audiences, and educational institutions will need to define their services to support these new noninstitutional career paths.

The true digital natives will value unfiltered-spectrum demographics. Demographic categories have long been used for everything from market segmentation to school admission policies. But segmentation based on *categories* like age, ethnicity, gender, health, and geography will give way to *spectrum* identities as high-resolution science reveals that even the most fundamental genetic markers measure a spectrum of characteristics—a spectrum that defeats simple categories such as male. vs. female, or Caucasian vs. African vs. Asian. At the same time, algorithmic matching software and vast personal databases are delivering on the promise of highly personalized products, services, and experiences, creating new expectations—and new challenges—for learners, workers, and organizations.

The proliferation of identity data is creating a need to create a portable portfolio of learning credentials, many of which are captured in real time from daily life. Educational institutions will have an opportunity to take the lead in defining the frameworks for capturing and accrediting these real-time credentials as well as creating the platforms for learners to monitor and share their profiles.

The challenge is to create personal brands that make their competencies known in a market of billions of category-defying individuals. Educational institutions are beginning to offer services that build on learner records. Employers are faced with the challenge of recruiting across international populations that are difficult to categorize. The challenge will be to design predictive modeling systems that target candidates who meet future spectrums of need. Organizations need to integrate platforms for recruiting from their own worker-learner networks.

The true digital natives will thrive in shape-shifting organizations. For centuries, societies have organized themselves around centralized and often hierarchical organizations that have promised stability, efficiency, productivity, and cultural cohesiveness. But distributed infrastructures—many based on distributed network technologies—are allowing people to organize their activities on scales that are both much smaller and much larger than centralized corporate-style structures. Distributed organizations are mastering the art of shape-shifting.

In an era of distributed computing, people must reimagine themselves so that they can perform a flexible mix of tasks. Educational institutions likewise need to redesign their own organizational structures to take advantage of distributed autonomous organizations and smart contracts in ways that implement the values expressed in their mission statements.

The extremely rapid organizing by young people from Marjory Stoneman Douglas High School in Parkland, Florida, after the awful shooting in February of 2018 is a dramatic example. Here's how journalist Dave Cullen, who also covered the Columbine shooting, described the rapid organizing that these true digital natives did on their own:

> Emma González called BS. David Hogg called out Adult America. The uprising had begun. Cameron Kasky immediately recruited a colorful band of theater kids and rising activists and brought them together

in his living room to map out a movement. Four days after escaping Marjory Stoneman Douglas High School, two dozen extraordinary kids announced the audacious March for Our Lives. A month later, it was the fourth-largest protest in American History.[4]

Another dramatic example is Greta Thunberg, a Swedish girl who is on the autism spectrum. At age 15 she seeded a global movement against climate disruption called Fridays for Future. In less than one year, she had millions of students walking out of school on Fridays, she spoke at the World Economic Forum in Davos, and she was nominated for the Nobel Peace Prize. When a true digital native can spread this kind of message so quickly and so powerfully, something is clearly changing.

The true digital natives will believe they are masterminds of their own reality. We are rapidly rewiring our planet with digital sensors and networks, creating a digital reality composed of "digital twins" that mirror humans and physical objects. These digital realities allow us to simulate both near- and long-term futures, challenging the world to build a widespread simulation literacy designed to empower everyone to participate in these control systems of the future. Often, they will value experiences over things. Often, they will choose to share, rent, or subscribe—rather than to buy.

Simulation literacy must become a core of a general education rather than a technical specialty, and this literacy will need to spread across K–12 institutions. Partnering among educational institutions and technology companies will be needed to build the foundational simulation tools and engage with employers to coinvent diverse simulation career paths. Learners now come to universities with an increasingly gameful mindset characterized by emotionally laden attention and an expectation of elegant and powerful blended-reality interfaces for learning. The early disappointments of educational gaming will be left behind.

Workplace simulations are challenging workers to master new ways of learning, collaborating and managing tasks and systems. Educational institutions have an opportunity to coinvent the new career paths for the simulated world—alongside in-simulation learning services that help students thrive in the simulated workplace. Simulation literacy will challenge organizations to design digital twins for all their assets and processes and to use these control systems for the physical world.

The true digital natives are very good at full-spectrum thinking, even though their brains—like all of us—are constantly trying to put things in categories. The true digital natives will challenge the social order.

When I've reviewed drafts of this chapter with a wide range of groups, I've often gotten a question something like this: "I get what you're saying about kids, but doesn't this just apply in Silicon Valley?" Indeed, Silicon Valley kids get access to better technology, tools, and networks than those in other parts of the world. On the other hand, no matter how poor a child is—even if hungry and hopeless—it is likely that they have some access to digital media already, and in 10 years that access will be pretty good anywhere on the planet. The rich kids will still have better access to connectivity, but even the poor kids will be pretty connected. If those connected poor kids have hope, that connectivity could be very positive. If not, those same kids could become candidates to join terrorist groups.

Many of the true digital natives globally will be asset poor, as I described in Chapter 3. Some of these same kids will have untreated childhood trauma, much of which could link to their poverty. Recent research has shown that untreated childhood trauma leads to major health and well-being challenges later in life. The Adverse Childhood Experiences (ACE) Study produced two striking findings: First, adverse childhood experiences are incredibly common in the United States—67 percent (two out of three people) of the study population had at least one, and 13 percent (one out of eight people) of the population had four or more adverse experiences. Second, there was a direct link to numerous health problems. This means that the more adverse experiences a child has, the higher is their risk of developing chronic illnesses such as heart disease, chronic obstructive pulmonary disease (COPD), depression, and cancer.[5]

Institute for the Future did a recent global study of youth in Austin, Mexico City, Berlin, Lagos, Jeddah, and Chongqing.[6] Our focus was on global youth skills for work and learning. Our findings support the forecast above and show that the true digital natives are a global phenomenon—although there are significant regional and local differences.

It is possible that the 2010 threshold prompted by the iPhone and iPad will be superseded by a new technology threshold that alters the neuroscience, sociology, and psychology of kids. We don't see these thresholds until we look back on them, but my guess is that we will look back on 2020 as another threshold year because new virtual, mixed, augmented, and blended-reality media are becoming much more usable and much less expensive. Young people who start to become adults in these new blended realities will be even more different than what I'm now calling the true digital natives, but we just don't yet know how. The next threshold may mark the "XR natives," named for their superpowers in moving across realities.

These future forces will shape the true digital natives as they become adults, so I want this chapter to frame the remainder of the book. The true digital natives will indeed make the future, and it will require broad-spectrum thinking to understand and work with them.

The true digital natives resist categorization (many of them are full-spectrum thinkers already), and the trendy term *Gen Z* is way too simplistic. The true digital natives can only be accurately described as a spectrum, not a category or a cohort. Generalizing across an entire generation has always been debatable, but to box in the true digital natives is just not accurate. They are a wild mix and they have the potential to change the world. Already today, digitally savvy young people can make a good living on gig work platforms without ever having a traditional job. The true digital natives see a spectrum of work and life options, not a yes/no job choice. The most elite of them may never have a job and yet be able to live very well.

The first true digital natives are just beginning to arrive in the workforce, and they will change the world. I'm very optimistic about the true digital natives, if they have hope.

PART THREE

BROADER SPECTRUMS, NEW APPLICATIONS FOR THE FUTURE

ORGANIZATIONS—ESPECIALLY BUSINESSES BUT ALSO NON-profits, government agencies, and the military—will have growing requirements for full-spectrum thinking and full-spectrum leadership. Leaders will face unnecessary and increasing risks if they get stuck evaluating new experiences through dirty old categorical filters.

Fortunately, new spectrums of innovation are beginning to appear already. Full-spectrum thinking will become the norm.

Part Three introduces five new spectrums of business and social value that are possible now and will scale over the next decade. Products will morph into services, subscriptions, and experiences. Ultimately, great products should incite personal transformations. Organization charts will become animated. What we call HR will transform into a Human-Computing Resources (HCR) function as powerful blending of humans, computing, and robotics becomes mainstream in the workforce. Diversity will be correlated with innovation. New spectrums of meaning will become possible.

It's too late to catch up, but it's a great time to leapfrog. These chapters introduce the unfolding story:

Chapter 7
Broader Spectrums of Business and Social Value
Operating in a Post-Categorical Distributed-Authority Future

Chapter 8
Broader Spectrums of Hierarchy
New Animated Organization Charts

Chapter 9
Broader Spectrums of Human–Machine Symbiosis
The New HR Will Be HCR

Chapter 10
Broader Spectrums of Diversity
New Inclusive Paths to Innovation

Chapter 11
Broader Spectrums of Meaning
A New Game of Hope

What will we call these next-generation full-spectrum innovations? The words we use to describe the future will have a big impact on our own ability to imagine that future. If we choose the right words, they will draw us toward that future. *Internet* and *World Wide Web* were wonderful terms that drew us toward the future. *Artificial intelligence* was the worst term to describe an emerging future that I have ever studied in my career. The term *artificial intelligence* invited horseless carriage thinking and fears of computers replacing or turning against humans.

If we choose the wrong words, we will fight the future. Right now, we're often stuck in the "eternal present" that neuroscientists tell us our brains crave. Old-fashioned categories expressed in worn-out words limit our ability to imagine the future. Our past limits our future. Full-spectrum thinking draws us toward the future. Broad-spectrum thinking is what we need, even if we cannot go all the way to full spectrum. The ideal future will be an intelligent blend of cautious categorical and disciplined full-spectrum thinking. Some people practice full-spectrum thinking already, even though they are in a categorical world with crude tools that skew strongly toward categorization.

In the classic futures movie *The Matrix*, the hero, Neo, is fighting an evil computing environment that is seemingly omniscient but is also limited by rules and categories. Neo, a human who is augmented by computers, has full-spectrum thinking capabilities that are physical and spiritual, in addition to his digital tools. In one critical scene, Neo goes to meet a wise person called the Oracle, and he encounters children who are bending spoons with their minds in the waiting area. These children appear to be understudies of the Oracle. One spoon-bending child advises Neo:

Do not try to bend the spoon,
that's impossible.
Instead, only try to realize the truth....
There is no spoon [emphasis added].
Then you'll see
that it is not the spoon that bends,
it is only yourself.[1]

Here's the gist: you can hold something you think of as a spoon in your hand, but there is no "spoon," just as there are no categories, labels, buckets, or boxes. The truth is there is only a spectrum of life experiences that we categorize to try to understand. The categories are fictional approximations, but the spectrum of experience is real. The categories themselves don't change; we must change ourselves. Full-spectrum thinking involves freeing ourselves from the constraints of categories.

Certainly, some people and some functions are already deeply engaged in full-spectrum thinking—and some have sophisticated digital support already. For example, a fighter pilot friend of mine tells me how, while flying, he needed to train his mind for parallel processing, not just sequential processing. He had to think about many things at once, across spectrums of possibility. Visualization, he says, is how he prepared himself to fly in this ever-changing multidimensional computer-enhanced world. During each flight, there are hundreds of data points for a pilot to scan continuously: instrument scans, altitude scans, heading, air space, and so on. There is always something to do, and they are flying so fast that there isn't much time at all to do them.

As my military pilot friends have explained to me, fighter pilots are trained with a timeline- and checklist-oriented approach, but they flex dynamically from this base and practice to the point of developing muscle and habit memory. This ability manifests in an ability to respond very quickly—sometimes without thinking at all. Successful fighter pilots are said to have "500-knot brains."

Contrast this with helicopter pilots, who do not need to adjust to the speed of decision making that fighter jets require but who require a different kind of dexterity. Successful helicopter pilots are said to have "50-knot brains."

This rings true to me as a former basketball player, although the slowest helicopter pilot's responses to challenges are probably faster than the fastest moves I ever made as a basketball player. The emerging tools will give many more of us 500-knot augmented human brains that will allow us to make sense out of the full-spectrum future that is emerging. They will help us seek new patterns and new clarity.

Certainly, others experience full-spectrum challenges that go beyond the checklists—in emergency rooms, for example. In the future scramble, many more of us will need this ability. Meanwhile, the dangers of simplistic overcategorization or premature categorization will loom. We can't slow down the game, but we can prepare better for it.

The future will force us to learn how to categorize with care and only after considering a continuum of possibilities. Fortunately, the emerging tools will help a lot and harm only a little. Full-spectrum thinking will be mostly good news, but there will be pitfalls, and they will be an important part of this book as well.

Organizations will have to change quickly in the scramble. Organization charts will become animated and shape-shifting. Leaders will face unnecessary and increasing risks if they get stuck evaluating new opportunities or risks through the filter of old categories that no longer work.

Just in time, new tools will make it much easier to think beyond the categories, labels, buckets, slots, and boxes that people use every day to filter their experiences of life—including threats and opportunities. Even though we cannot predict the future, we can do a lot better than blindly throwing the future into buckets from the past. Categorization is not just saying what something is; it is saying what it is not. Carving the future into categories from the past will be risky business. Full-spectrum inclusion will help organizations realize that diversity correlates with innovation.

Full-spectrum thinking will help people avoid thoughtless labeling of people or experiences with old categories, buckets, slots, boxes, stereotypes, or generalizations. It will be a technology-enabled antidote to polarization.

Priority Questions for Part Three

As an individual, how can you explore and try out new approaches to full-spectrum thinking in your daily lifestyle, your vocation, and your personal sense of meaning? How can you rethink your old habits and consider new lifestyle or mindset options?

As an organization, how can you design and prototype full-spectrum thinking in your business models, your organizational structure, and your human-computing resource activities? How can you develop the link between diversity and innovation?

How can societies incentivize and prototype regulations in ways that encourage broad thinking about possibilities for the future and moderate stereotyping of those that don't fit societal norms?

CHAPTER 7

Broader Spectrums of
Business and Social Value

Operating in a Post-Categorical
Distributed-Authority Future

A YOUNG SOFTWARE ENGINEER IN SILICON VALLEY WAS surprised when the CIO called him aside to tell him that his company was giving him a performance bonus of $100,000, the largest spot bonus his company had ever given to anyone. The young engineer left the office stunned. Even during a boom period in Silicon Valley, this bonus was exceptional.

The executive told the young man that he was giving him the bonus because he wanted him to stay with the company for a very long time. He assumed that the young man would use his bonus for a down payment on a house in Silicon Valley, or to buy a Tesla.

The following Monday morning, the young man came to the executive to say that he really appreciated the bonus and that he would be using it to backpack in Europe until he had spent all the money. He was leaving the company. When he returned to the Bay Area, he said, he hoped he might return to the firm. He was very appreciative of the bonus.

The executive was stunned until he realized that the experience of backpacking was more important to this young person than physical things that the bonus could buy.

Ten years from now, valuing experiences over things will be pervasive as the true digital natives become adults and take on leadership roles in the world of work. In Chapter 6, I discussed how digital natives often value experience more than things. Many of them are skeptical about the value of owning things and sophisticated about how the sharing economy can work for them. We just don't know how rapidly an experiential mindset will spread.

The most profitable ways of doing business in the future will be to deliver transformative services and experiences—for shoppers and for larger social good—not just to sell products. Products will still be foundational, but products alone will be increasingly commoditized, and the most profitable businesses will be wrapping products in compelling experiences. Increasingly, people will make carefully informed choices between what they want to own and what they just want to use.

This shift from things to services is happening even in the business-to-business world—not just in consumer products.

In the fall of 2016, I spoke at a CEO forum in Washington, DC, and met Michael Kneeland, then the CEO of United Rentals—the world's largest rental equipment company. I knew nothing about the equipment rental business at the time, and I must admit that I didn't expect it to be very interesting or future oriented. My views since then have changed dramatically. Equipment rental is a signal of what is to come, and United Rentals is much farther down the path than others. United Rentals knows how to help people use very sophisticated machines without having to buy them.

What Do You Need to Use but Do Not Need to Own?

Consider the large metal plates that cover holes in any construction site. They clank as you drive over them, but they protect you from falling into a hole. Those plates are very large, very expensive, and very difficult to move. You rarely need them and you certainly wouldn't want to own one, but during construction they are absolutely necessary. Metal plates are a perfect rental product, but they are just the beginning of this story.

United Rentals rents equipment like air compressors, scissor lifts, boom lifts, towable light towers, track loaders, reach forklifts, portable generators, heaters, vertical lifts, backhoes, mini-excavators, welders, and many more. On most large construction sites in the United States, you are likely to see United Rentals equipment. This equipment is vital during construction, but after the job is done, most people don't want or need a reach forklift or a mini-excavator. Renting makes much more sense than owning construction equipment. Even if you are constructing large buildings, you have no interest in owning your own reach forklift. You only want to *use* the reach forklift to build your building, and then you don't want it around anymore. As the old saying goes, when you go to buy a drill or a drill bit, what you really want to buy is a hole.

The massive equipment that United Rentals rents can do amazing things in the hands of a skilled operator, but it is dangerous in the hands of someone inexperienced. Safety on the jobsite is worth a lot, in addition to the functionality of the equipment. Beyond products, United Rentals is providing solutions that include use of those products during the time when they are needed. United Rentals offers a spectrum of products, services, and experiences for products that you need but may not want to own or learn how to operate. They train your equipment operators or provide operators for the equipment you rent. Most importantly given the size and dangers of this equipment, they provide safety services.

United Rentals is now focusing on the construction worker of the future, which will certainly be a blend of human and robotic resources. United Rentals is military friendly and has been a large-scale donor of exoskeletons for wounded warriors. Now, the company is using exoskeleton technologies to arm the superempowered construction worker. Again, the focus is on providing not just the product but services and experiences to get big jobs done productively and safely. The superempowered construction worker will be a cyborg of incredible power and flexibility. United Rentals is becoming a service business, and other industries will learn from its innovation.

The Shift from Products to Experiences

For almost 10 years now, I have been teaching at what was first called EA University and is now known as Electronic Arts in Redwood Shores, EARS, or just EA, one of the world's largest video game publishing companies. I work with the rising star leaders, helping them figure out how to thrive in the emerging future world.

When I began teaching at EA University, they had just hired one of my former clients from Procter & Gamble who had been working on the Walmart account for P&G. Just as Walmart was one of P&G's largest customers, it was one of EA's largest customers. EA hired my friend Doug Bowser from P&G because he knew how to sell to Walmart, even though EA was selling video games and not consumer products.

Ten years ago, Electronic Arts sold most of their games in boxes at retail outlets like Walmart. Now, they are selling games online through subscription services to player networks. They are delivering experiences to a network of gamers, not just selling a game in a box. For players and for EA, the spectrum of value is increasing. Characters within games, for example, have become a substantial source of revenue for EA and other gaming companies. You no longer buy a game; you sign up for an ongoing gaming experience. Doug Bowser is now president and chief operating officer of Nintendo of America.

· In the next decade, most companies will have to shift toward offering services and experiences in order to make reasonable profit. Industries like information technology, transportation, retail, health care, and housing will follow ways of doing business that are like those of United Rentals and Electronic Arts today. Even very traditional industries will be disrupted.

When I was 16 years of age growing up in rural Illinois, I was totally focused on getting my driver's license and owning a car. I thought I wanted a car, but in retrospect I realize that I just wanted to drive and be seen driving. For most 16-year-olds today, it is more about mobility than cars. Why would they want to *own* a car?

At Institute for the Future, we have worked over the years with almost all of the car manufacturers. Automakers are core to the world's economy, with a long history of producing products in assembly lines. I noticed a few years ago that the car makers who visited IFTF were introducing themselves as providers of mobility services, rather than car makers. As the automotive industry has developed, the goal has been to sell a car to every person or at least every family. The cars themselves are distributed broadly, but up until recently they haven't been connected. In a future where everything that can be distributed will be distributed, cars will be both distributed and connected. Car-sharing services, Uber, and Lyft are prototyping the kind of mobility services that will become possible as car products evolve into mobility services.

Joe Pine and Jim Gilmore were prescient when they wrote the first edition of their book *The Experience Economy*[1] in 1999. They argued that the macroeconomic shift would be from products to services to experiences. They used examples like Disney and Hallmark to make their case, and it was a convincing case even then. Now, what Pine and Gilmore first called the "experience economy" is finally beginning to scale globally. The experience economy, whatever it comes to be called, will include a spectrum of value leading toward personal and organizational transformation.

Amazon has been a major disruptor in the acceleration of commoditization. Amazon has made it harder and harder for others to make money selling products alone. Easy online shopping is leading to extreme price pressures and the commoditization of anything that can be commoditized. When you are competing on price alone, there will be little profit margin. If there are no margins, scale doesn't help. As I will describe in Chapter 8 in more detail, economies of scale will yield to economies of organization. Companies will be what they can organize profitably and sustainably.

While products can be commoditized, it is much harder and sometimes impossible to commoditize services or experiences or transformations. Also, the profit margins on services and experiences are much higher than the margins on products alone.

Meanwhile the online infrastructure for services and experiences is becoming much more powerful. Businesses will be challenged to provide a much wider spectrum of value offerings as it gets harder and harder to make profit from selling products alone.

The Shift from Experiences to Transformations

Transformations can be personal or organizational. The overall economic shift will be from commodities to products to services to experiences to personal transformations. It will be increasingly difficult to make money from products alone. The most successful companies will create memorable experiences that incite personal or organizational transformations.

Walt Disney World was one of the core examples of the experience economy that Pine and Gilmore cited in *The Experience Economy*. I first worked with John Padgett at Walt Disney World in Orlando, when he was on the team that created the Magic Band. The prototype I carried was called Pal Mickey, and it had a sensor in its nose so it could tell me where I was in the park at any time.

Pal Mickey gave me guidance about where the lines were shorter as I moved around and what I might like to see. It told me canned jokes in between suggestions. Pal Mickey didn't quite work out, but it failed in an interesting way since it led to the graceful Magic Band of today that has turned Walt Disney World into a giant computer designed to make the guest experience easier and more profound. Prototypes are messy, but at Walt Disney World, nothing is messy to the guest.

The cruise industry is now picking up on the innovations that began in theme parks. John Padgett was recruited from Walt Disney World to Carnival Corporation to be their chief innovation and experience officer, to lead the team that created the world's first digital cruise ship. Where Disney is more hierarchical, Carnival is more distributed. Padgett and his team brought the anytime-anyplace guest experience to cruise ships, which is an environment where services and experiences can be delivered in an even more focused way than within a theme park.

Before the trip, guests provide all the information about themselves, their families, and their preferences that they choose to provide, in return for dramatically personal experiences while they are on board. All of their preferences are encoded in a medallion that they carry on board at all times. You can wear it around your neck, on a wrist band, or embedded in a variety of jewelry items that are sold by Carnival.

The giant ships have sensors implanted about every 10 feet on all the decks. The MedallionClass Princess Cruise ships have become giant computers that just happen to look like ships and sail anywhere. Once you are on board wearing your medallion, services and experiences are delivered in very personal and very customized ways—as long as you give away clues about yourself before you come on board and agree to share your data while on board. For example, no need for keys to your stateroom, no need for credit cards for food or drinks, in gift shops, or at the casino. An OceanCompass enables dynamic wayfinding throughout the ship (the ships are so large that I find this feature particularly useful). An interactive timeline lets guests scroll through all events available, and all the events are matched to the location of the guest on board.

On board, guests can buy products, but what they are really paying for is the experience. The best cruise lines are selling transformative family or personal experiences that are so wonderful that the guests forget how much they paid. What guests are buying is the overall experience, and the more personalized the experience is, the more powerful the transformation—and the more they are willing to pay. What is the family experience of a lifetime worth? Successful experiences are also very hard to copy. Experiences are monetized in a variety of services and products purchased while on board. A high-margin experience can include many low margin products if the guest experience remains the priority.

John Padgett describes what Carnival Corporation is seeking for the guests:

> We are focused with extreme clarity on giving our guests more of what they liked before but taking away what they didn't. We want their experience to be customized and we want to absorb the complexity so that each guest gets an experience that is personalized, frictionless, and immersive.[2]

In the early days of Disneyland and Walt Disney World, it was possible to have an "on stage" and a "back stage," in order to create a great guest experience. Now that guests come into the park or onto the ship so digitally connected, it is nearly impossible to hide the "back stage." The connectivity has to create an environment of options where every guest feels empowered and in control. You want to avoid any feelings of privacy violation, but it's easier to do on board a ship, since people can select how much of their personal data and preferences they want to share. The more personal data that guests choose to share, the richer the experience on board the ship will be for them. Both Walt Disney World and Carnival Corporation are embracing what I would call full-spectrum thinking about the business offerings they provide.

Why Not Subscribe to a Product?

In his book *Subscribed*, the founder and CEO of Zuora, Tien Tzuo (an early employee at Salesforce), outlined the shift away from the product economy to the new subscription economy. "The end of ownership" is his company's mantra. His thesis is that "the pure product economy is nearing the end of a 120-year run and the world is shifting towards services." Of course, products are still owned by somebody, but who owns the products will shift dramatically. Here are the core shifts that Tzuo is forecasting:

Pricing: *from* unit sales *toward* value pricing

Marketing: *from* branding *toward* experience

Sales: *from* selling products *toward* selling outcomes

Finance: *from* unit margins *toward* customer lifetime value

Culture: *from* hit products *toward* deep relationships

These are the same kinds of shifts that Pine and Gilmore forecasted more than 20 years ago. The subscription economy provides infrastructure for the experience economy. Over the next decade, the experience economy will become scalable and sustainable. It will also become a competitive game changer in many industries.

I love Tzuo's story of how Fender started using Zuora and created a subscription service aimed at supporting a lifetime of guitar playing. When I bought my first guitar many years ago while I was in graduate school, I didn't have much money but certainly knew about and valued the Fender brand. I still have a Fender 12-string, but I've only bought guitars and I haven't (yet) subscribed to a guitar-playing service. I'm brand loyal to Fender in the sense that I've always loved the brand and I'm proud of my Fender, but the company has gotten very little from my loyalty—except for my initial purchase a long time ago.

What Fender has now realized is that many people buy a first guitar but never really learn how to play it. Many people stop playing after the first few months. What if, instead of just buying a guitar, people subscribed to a guitar player's service? For beginners, the focus would be on tuning and learning how to play the first few chords. For advanced users, the services could expand greatly and link to communities of guitar players with similar tastes in music, similar skill levels, and similar interests in learning. Buying a guitar is just a first step in the experience of playing a guitar. The value for Fender can be a continuing value, just as the experience of the guitar player can grow. Guitar playing can become a transformative experience that lasts a lifetime—and now it can be a Fender-branded experience.

On Sunday, June 9, 2019, the Sunday Styles section of *The New York Times* ran this headline on a story about how many young American urbanites are choosing to rent rather than own:

> Let's Subscribe to That Sofa: Owning nothing is now
> a luxury, thanks to a number of rental startups[3]

The fashionable young woman featured in her Los Angeles apartment was shown with her rented sofa, coffee table, shirt, dress, jacket, lamp, and bed frame. Increasingly, people will be able to decide (and no longer just assume) what they want to own and what they want to just use. New services, subscriptions, and experiences will increase the range of choices.

United Rentals does something similar by giving customers telematics units to install on their own equipment so that they can get the same United Rentals experience even when not renting from United Rentals.

Zuora is a signal of a subscription-based future that is already here, but unevenly distributed. Platforms like Zuora have the potential to facilitate spectrum thinking about products and services and subscriptions. Platforms like this suggest ways of doing business and then provide media for bringing them to life.

The Silicon Valley company Peloton has broken new ground by turning home exercise equipment into a transformative experience:

> Peloton doesn't see itself as being in the fitness business, which is crowded with competitors. [John] Foley and his team see themselves as being in the *fitness experience* business, which is distinct and differentiated. Peloton sees itself in the relationship building business as well. Customers get to know their instructors personally and become part of each other's lives. As they compete with other cyclists spinning remotely in their homes and apartments, Peloton sells the motivation and the energy of a live spin class. And Peloton gains data with which to constantly improve further.
>
> Unlike other manufacturers of stationary bikes, Peloton doesn't just sell equipment. Using the "razor and blades" business model popularized by Gillette, Peloton sells "razors" (stationary bikes) and "blades" in the

form of monthly subscriptions to online classes, in addition to a widening array of new revenue streams to a captive audience. The monthly subscription model entitles users to online classes as well as other classes, from strength training to stretching and high intensity interval routines.[4]

When I bought my first home exercise bike in San Francisco in 1979, I had to order it through a boxing gymnasium in order to get a high-quality bike. Now, retail stores make it easy to buy high-quality equipment. Peloton is making it easy to subscribe to a high-quality experience that just happens to include a bike. Whether or not Peloton succeeds commercially, they are a signal of what is to come.

Business services like these will accelerate the spread of the experience economy, and they will be amplified by distributed-authority networks. What we think of today as blockchain, for example, will provide platforms for a new spectrum of value offerings at the intersection of money, technology, and human identity. In Institute for the Future's forecast of blockchain futures, done in 2017 and looking out to 2027, we outlined three waves of change from currencies to computing to commons. Each will provoke application spaces where new ways of doing business will become possible.

Finding Your Organization's Opportunity Zones

Below are key innovation zones to explore in order to imagine new services, subscriptions, and transformative experiences. I've included questions you can ask yourself about new spectrums of value that your organization might provide.

Ten years from now, how will you track new identity credentials and metrics to reduce friction and increase the value you provide? A key question here is who owns what data. Increasingly, individual people are concerned about their own data and how it might be used against them. This concern can be flipped into an opportunity if companies can figure out how to provide value that links back to personal data. The higher ground is to give people choices with regard to their own data.

How might you create new spectrums of value by monetizing an asset you already own but are not utilizing? In the book I wrote with P&G

innovation icon Karl Ronn called *The Reciprocity Advantage,*[5] we explored ways in which companies can give away underutilized assets and partner to create new businesses that they could not create on their own. Distributed-authority computing will provide dramatic new opportunities for reciprocity-based innovation. The key is to determine your right of way in a new business opportunity zone and what underutilized asset you have that can be used to seed innovation and growth.

How might you and your competitors offer new value by ensuring that supply web or other records have not been changed before they reach your customer? Trust is basic and these new systems *should* instill trust and improve trustworthiness. Expect a new spectrum of services that help people manage their own digital identities to both add value and reduce risk. Can transparent access to a shared history of custody help you trust collaborators? Blockchain and other distributed platforms will provide new ways to track and verify the history of transactions over time. These systems have the potential to reduce risk and bring trusted computing to low-trust environments. The vision here is of a distributed unchangeable ledger that is continuous and trustworthy.

Will you be able to reduce the need for trusted third parties by taking advantage of new digital smart contract capabilities? Integrity and trust will be automated in distributed-authority computing environments, but it is still not clear how long this will take and just how much built-in integrity and trust will be possible. There is still a tension between the vision and the reality, but this will be sorted out over the next decade to a much greater extent than we see now.[6]

What's Next?

Distributed autonomous organizations (DAOs) will become possible over the next decade, and the wild card is how successful they will be, how rapidly they will grow and multiply. A DAO is a company owned and operated by an algorithm, rather than one or more humans. In a DAO, authority could be distributed across a network of digital resources.

Imagine that large machines owned themselves, rented themselves out, and hired humans to repair them. Why would the machines need, or customers want, United Rentals? United Rentals has a very good answer to that question: personal service, safety, and productivity that allow the customers to achieve the outcomes they desire. United Rentals provides an overall service that customers value.

In the future, will there be portions of your business that could be done successfully by a DAO? What other industries are vulnerable to such a challenge?

On-demand match-making services like Uber could evolve into a wide array of internet-connected mobility devices with distributed-authority connectivity that links riders with vehicles. Vehicles could be dispatched with algorithmic efficiency. What extra value would the human-led company provide? The answer isn't obvious to me.

Digital networks will force down profit margins and turn many products into low- or no-margin commodities. They will also introduce a spectrum of new business opportunities with much higher margins focusing on services, subscriptions, experiences, and personal or organizational transformations. Expect new spectrums of value for individuals, organizations, and society. For individuals, experiences will increase in value. For organizations, expect an evolution from products to experiences to personal transformations. For societies and cultures, shared assets (like water and air quality) will become more explicitly offered.

CHAPTER 8

Broader Spectrums
of Hierarchy

New Animated Organization Charts

THE WEEK BEFORE 9/11, I WAS INVITED WITH A GROUP OF Deloitte senior partners to spend three days at the Army War College and on the Gettysburg Battlefield to discuss strategy and leadership in the future. This was my first experience at the graduate school for the US Army in Carlisle, Pennsylvania.

As a young man, I had a very limited military background (only a year of required ROTC at the University of Illinois when I was an undergraduate), and I came to the Army War College with low expectations. I expected that the Army would be very hierarchical and rigid, command-and-control.

It turned out, to my utter surprise, that the three-day staff ride was life changing for me. I was wrong about the Army. Parts of the Army are still hierarchical, I have learned, but not in the sense that I had expected. The Army now has spectrums of hierarchy in its various organizations. The Army is prototyping a future where hierarchies are no longer static; they will be animated. Command-and-control only works in predictable slow-moving environments, and there aren't very many of those any more.

Beyond Command-and-Control

Instead of the old command-and-control, the Army now practices what they call "commander's intent," "mission command," or "flexive command."[1] Wharton business school professor Michael Useem describes *commander's intent* in this way: "The commander did not say *how*, but he unequivocally conveyed *what*." *Mission command* is similar, but broader: "Given the tactical, operational, and strategic context, how should I command?" Direction is very clear; execution is very flexible. Hierarchies are still present, but they come and go. Old-fashioned hierarchies just don't work as well anymore because the external world is changing so quickly—and it is not just in the military.

The latest term, which I've come to prefer but which is not used broadly yet, is *flexive command*,[2] which requires leaders to be very clear where they want to go, but very flexible about how they get there. Situation analysis (being very aware of surroundings, context, and shifts) is required to continuously evaluate who is in the best position to make which decision at what time.

I have been told many times by Army friends that the transformation of the Army from command-and-control started in Vietnam, where it became apparent that warfare was even more asymmetric and unpredictable than in the past. Asymmetric jungle warfare required asymmetric ways of organizing for combat. In the Vietnam War, I am told, command-and-control hierarchies just didn't work well.

This latest shift from symmetrical warfare (where the enemy wore uniforms and fought stylistically according to generally agreed-upon practices of war) to asymmetrical warfare (where unstructured guerrilla warfare was the norm) began in Vietnam but is becoming much more complex now. A long complicated evolutionary change ensued for the Army as they created new kinds of hierarchy.

Commander's intent, which was originally developed by the military, is surfacing in various forms across the spectrum of organizations. In Chapter 7, for example, I described a range of companies that are shifting from selling products to selling services and experiences. Each of them has a compelling equivalent of commander's intent, although they don't use military language explicitly.

What Is Your Commander's Intent?

On Carnival's digital cruise ships, their commander's intent is to focus relentlessly on the guest experience. The goal is to be personalized, frictionless, and immersive. They want to absorb the complexity of the experience for the guest, so the guest can enjoy it and be transformed.

At Electronic Arts, their commander's intent is "we exist to inspire the world to play."

At United Rentals, their commander's intent builds on their mission: "to serve customers with excellence," with a constant emphasis on both productivity and safety. Their business requires safety first because the risk of accidents is profound with large equipment.

These types of corporate mission statements only work if they somehow carry down to day-to-day decisions in the business. Commander's intent must guide behavior through the complexities of daily life. Again, be very clear about where you are going—but very flexible about how you get there. The complexities, however, are getting even more complex, and that is likely to continue into the future. Hierarchical organizations are just too brittle to function well in extreme complexity.

Around the time of the 2016 presidential election, Yaneer Bar-Yam, director of the New England Complex Systems Institute, commented that we had reached the limits of hierarchical organizations. He questioned whether any presidential candidate could lead organizations as complex as we have become. Essentially, our organizations have become too complex to manage with hierarchies. "We've become fundamentally confused about what the decisions are, and what their consequences are."[3]

Hierarchies only work up to a certain limit of complexity, which we have now surpassed.

Clarity is hierarchical with regard to direction, but it is also very adaptive to unforeseen circumstances. The military is ahead of business in this shift toward animated hierarchies, which is why I've become so intrigued by what they are learning—while still realizing all the extreme challenges that they face.

After Action Reviews

Commander's intent works much better if lessons from the field are understood and acted upon by leaders. The Army has developed a practice they call "after action reviews" (AARs), and they have implemented it on a very large scale. The idea is to build in a daily practice—a personal discipline, actually—that every significant activity will be debriefed and learned from after it happens. What happened? What worked well? What could be improved? While the results of AARs are catalogued and are sometimes useful to share, the real value is in the discipline, the ways of thinking and acting that include learning from experiences.

The key to successful AARs is to separate the organizational field experience from individual performance evaluation. It took a very long time, I've been told, for the Army to learn how to separate AARs from personal performance reviews. Certainly, AARs or reviews like them are used in many parts of many businesses, but this discipline has been very difficult to scale and sustain. In the world of business, I know many companies that use something like AARs in some parts of their organizations. I don't, however, know a single company using AARs that has separated them from personal performance reviews across the entire company. It is important that this process be done with a positive learning mindset. For some companies I have seen, the process is more a "postmortem" (probably not the best term) with a focus on the past than an organizational learning opportunity focused on the future.

Finally, situation awareness is key to commander's intent. Situation awareness is the ability to sense what is going on around you at all times. Simulation and gaming are the primary ways that people learn to develop their own situation awareness. The essence of flexive command is to use situation awareness to continuously evaluate who is in the best position to make which decision at what time. Again, all this assumes great *clarity of direction* and great *flexibility of execution*.

After 9/11, I was asked to help organize a series of exchanges between military, business, and nonprofit leaders to discuss the future of leadership, strategy, and learning. With Willie Pietersen from Columbia Business School, I organized some 15 of these exchanges with a wide range of leaders. Later, I was able to work with the new three-star generals on their first week in Washington, DC.

My books *Leaders Make the Future* and *The New Leadership Literacies* were both heavily influenced by my experiences at the Army War College and with military leaders. I have learned so much from them. These experiences have been a big part of my learning about organizations in the future. I believe that the life-and-death experiences of the military are a very important lead indicator of how to organize for the future.

Shape-Shifting Organizations

These principles provide a preview of the organization of the future where rigid hierarchical organization charts will yield to shape-shifting structures that will be not only flexible but animated. The animated org charts of the future will look something like the one in Figure 8.1.

Imagine that this graphic is undulating, with hierarchies moving up and down. That's what an animated org chart will look like, but most organizations aren't there yet. Even in the Army, there is still a traditional hierarchy that is very slow moving and bureaucratic—although the special forces are shape-shifting.

In the summer of 2018, the Army created a new Futures Command that is based in Austin and Virginia. This is how they describe their mission:

> The Directorate of Intelligence, Army Futures Command evaluates emerging threats, integrates the future operational environment, and shapes future capabilities and technologies for future investments to enable the development of requirements, capabilities, protection and delivery of concepts, and future force designs for Army Future Modernization.
>
> A team of teams will enable the Army to forecast the future, shape the changing character of war, and deliver intelligence capabilities that ensures the Army remains the pre-eminent fighting force in the world.[4]

In this remarkably candid document (more candid than what I see in public statements from most corporations), the Army acknowledges the urgency of their challenge and the need for speed:

> The Army's current requirements and capabilities development practices take too long. The Army is losing near-peer competitive advantage in

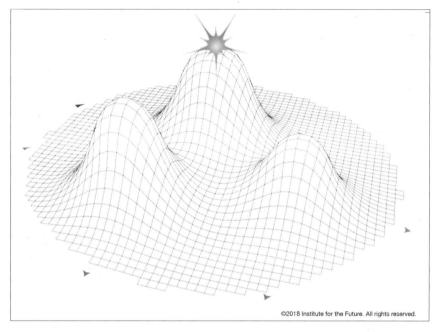

FIGURE 8.1 A visualization of an evolving shape-shifting organization that has no center, grows from the edges, has hierarchies that come and go, and cannot be controlled.

many areas: we are outranged, outgunned, and increasingly outdated. Private industry and some potential adversaries are fielding new capabilities much faster than we are. The speed of change in warfighting concepts, threats, and technology is outpacing current Army modernization constructs and processes.[5]

Furthermore, the Futures Command will "provide full spectrum protection"[6] for the United States in this climate of urgency. Companies need to take the same pledge of full-spectrum future readiness. But most companies, in my experience, don't yet have a strong enough sense of urgency or expertise to make this kind of pledge.

I showed the Figure 8.1 graphic about shape-shifting organizations to the CEO of a very large corporation recently, and he studied it with interest. I was in his very large office on the visitor's side of his very large desk. After a few minutes, he leaned across his desk and stuck his chin out at me while asking coarsely: "Where do *I* sit?"

His question caught me by surprise, but it was a very good one. I think that leaders sit at the foundation of shape-shifting organizations. Leaders will still be a source of clarity, but the leader will not always be on top. The source of clarity should be the grounding, and it should flow up and out across the network.

As we move into the future, this is a good time to rethink classic concepts of leadership like "leadership from behind"[7] and "servant leadership."[8] Organizational boundaries will be porous and opportunistic but linked by the clarity of core values and direction. Hierarchies will come and go as the needs change. There will be great flexibility to scale up and down. There will be more ways to make a living. But nobody will truly control these organizations. They can be guided, but they can't be controlled.

Shape-shifting organizations will be great for those workers who are ready for freelance work. On some gig work platforms already, it is possible for expert designers or programmers to make very good income, with health care benefits and retirement planning—while according to the US government, they won't have a "job" in the traditional sense.

For those not ready to make a living within the gig economy, however, this world will be close to slave labor: microtasks for micropennies. Inevitably in this increasingly dynamic world of work, there will be fewer traditional jobs and more potential for worker abuse. Any jobs that can be broken into pieces will be broken into pieces. Some unions will survive, but only if they are extremely innovative and adaptive.

The military is ahead of civilian organizations in moving toward shape-shifting structures, except for start-ups and innovation teams that live on the edges of large organizations. In general, smaller organizations are more shape-shifting than larger. And, the criminals are better at shape-shifting than the rest of us. When I show the shape-shifting organizational graphic in Figure 8.1 to military groups and ask them who it reminds them of, they immediately say terrorist groups. The criminals, in fact, are much better at shape-shifting organizations than the rest of us, and they have fewer constraints—like laws.

The Organization Chart of the Future

Traditional organization charts are hierarchical and static. Looking 10 years ahead, organization charts will be dynamic, and hierarchies will come and go. It won't be the end of hierarchy, but it will be the end of static hierarchy.

Animated organizations will have no center, they will grow from the edges (where diversity flourishes), hierarchies will come and go, and they won't be controllable. A spectrum of come-and-go hierarchies and distributed social networks will create many more ways of working.

To thrive, leaders will need new full-spectrum thinking capabilities and skills to make good use of the new tools I discussed in Chapter 3. Collective intelligence—humans working together, augmented by machines—will be required to thrive.

In the old world of hierarchical structures, bigger was almost always better. Looking 10 years ahead, you will be what you can organize. Economies of scale will yield to what I think of as economies of organization.

In 2018, a new book came out by Jeremy Heimans and Henry Timms that provides great insight about the shift toward animated organizations. They are both very experienced community organizers, and Henry Timms was one of the key people behind "Giving Tuesday" (the Tuesday after Thanksgiving Day in the US, established to encourage charitable giving across the world during the winter holiday season).

Their book title is revealing in itself: *New Power: How Power Works in Our Hyperconnected World—and How to Make It Work for You.* They argue that there is a clear directional shift from old power to new power. "New Power is the deployment of mass participation and peer coordination to create change and shift outcomes."[9] This is a book that explores the changing structure of power through the use of connective media and shape-shifting organizations.

Table 8.1 is a summary of the shift from old power to new power that they are forecasting, which is very consistent with my view.

In the book, Heimans and Timms give many examples of new-power organizations like populist political campaigns, Airbnb, and some cooperatives. The video game company Valve Corporation, for example, is organized around a "no managers" policy that allows employees to propose

TABLE 8.1 The Coming Power Shifts

Old Power	New Power
Currency	Current
Held by few	Made by many
Downloads	Uploads
Commands	Shares
Leader-driven	Peer-driven
Closed	Open

After Heimans and Timms, 2018.

and run their own workstreams independently of predefined structures like teams or divisions. It allows for fluid movement across the organization and self-regulating productivity within the company. Of course, this kind of shape-shifting organizational structure only works if there is compelling clarity of direction and values that are shared.

My forecast is that this shift from old power to new power will accelerate. The next generation of the internet will amplify distributed organizations without nearly as much central authority—which will mean a restructuring of power.

Organization charts can be animated virtually to reflect work that happens with a range of people with whom the company works—not just formal employees. Tasks will get built into the chart, and people will be able to explore formal and informal connections. This kind of organization chart can show hierarchies and formal structures, but it can also reflect informal communication patterns and who relies upon whom.

Organizations will be created very rapidly, sometimes with dramatic impact. Individuals, organizations, and society will be disrupted as we move beyond command-and-control. Much of the innovation in this emerging world comes from entrepreneurs, the military, and the criminals. Distributed-authority networks will mean fluid hierarchies that require constant reassessment of who is in the best position to make which decision at what time. Individuals will need to learn how to lead when they cannot control. Organizations will need to learn how to flex rapidly while retaining clarity of direction. Societies will need to create commons that benefit everyone, shared assets, and a decision-making process that helps people decide what they choose to do together.

In the animated shape-shifting organizations of the future, you will be what you can organize.

CHAPTER 9

Broader Spectrums of Human–Machine Symbiosis

The New HR Will Be HCR

THE CHESS GRANDMASTER GARRY KASPAROV REFLECTED on his 1997 loss to an IBM supercomputer program called Deep Blue:

> Today, May 11, 2017, marks the 20th anniversary of my loss against Deep Blue in our 1997 rematch in New York City....
>
> I spent much of last year working on a book, *Deep Thinking*, that includes my memories and analysis of that fateful match, the so-called Brain's Last Stand that turned me into the proverbial man in "man versus machine"....
>
> I make it clear in *Deep Thinking* that my loss to Deep Blue was also a victory for humans—its creators and everyone who benefits from our technological leaps. That is, everyone. This is always the case in the big picture, and why the book rejects the "man vs. machine" competition storyline. The machines work for us, after all.
>
> The last third of the book is about the bright future of our lives with intelligent machines, if we are ambitious enough to embrace it. I hope my optimism is contagious.[1]

Kasparov's reflection reveals that his personal defeat by the computer was an unexpected victory for humankind. His experience taught us that human–machine competition is not a zero-sum game. Rather, it is possible that both computers and humans can come out ahead. What can humans do best? What can computers do best? These crucial questions challenge us to explore the symbiosis between humans and machines. Over the next decade, this exploration will be more promising than ever before.

Technology organizations are already involved in this exploration, but the organizational function that is best equipped to answer these questions is what we call today "human resources." The best strategic human resources organizations already think about talent acquisition, performance management, employment data analytics, and ethics. I'm suggesting that human resources must now extend into the world of superminds.

Ten years from now, most of us will be superempowered cyborgs. What we call "human resources" today will be very different tomorrow as humans and computers become increasingly intermingled. A crucial gray scale will emerge on the spectrum from human to computer. What we call human resources today will, if they rise to the occasion, support what MIT professor Thomas W. Malone calls the "superminds" of tomorrow in his 2018 book *Superminds*:

> This book is not primarily about how computers will do things people used to do. It's about how people and computers together will do things that were never possible before. It's about how human-computer superminds will be smarter than anything our world has ever seen. And it's about how we can use these new kinds of collective intelligence to help solve some of our most important problems in business, government, and many other parts of society.[2]

Humans and Machines

Human resource professionals will need the ability to better understand the capabilities of nonhuman and computer-augmented talent. In fact, 10 years from now, most humans will be boosted by computing resources in some way. We will all be superminds.

Intelligent coworkers with powerful digital augmentation will be everywhere. Automation of routine functions will certainly happen, but the biggest disruptions will come from digitally amplified humans. The machines will be more human-centered, and the humans will be more digitally amplified. Most importantly, by looking at themselves in digital mirrors, humans will understand more deeply what humans do best and what it means to be human—as Garry Kasparov described above.

The US Navy's new ships are designed to make the best use of human-computing resources: the ships are more automated and the smaller numbers of human sailors are more generalist—less specialist:

> The whole ship had the feel of a small theatre troupe in which the actor playing the prince's cousin also plays the apothecary, the friar, and Messenger No. 2.[3]

These hybrid sailors change roles frequently and are augmented cyborgs at their core. While the humans are generalists, the computers are specialists. Some tasks are automated away (which can be problematic if things go wrong), and the humans are always augmented by digital resources. Cyborgs are everywhere on a modern US Navy ship.

The humans emphasize effectiveness (doing the right things), while the computers emphasize efficiency (doing things right). People with a rich range of life experiences will do best in this world. The challenge is to hold the balance between what humans do well and what computers do well in the midst of the continuing scramble of the external world.

If we can get our language to describe this emerging and transformative function right, it will draw us toward a better future. The future of HR should be a conversation about human-computing resources (HCR)—not conventional HR. There will be increasing need for alignment and collaboration between the CHRO, the CTO, and the CIO, the human and the machine intelligence.

Separating human and computing resources will be increasingly difficult. The power and productivity will be in augmentation of what humans do best and what computers do best. It is already too late to have a "digital strategy." Now, organizations need strategy that includes digital. Indeed, the word *digital* will gradually disappear, since digital media will be so pervasive. When digital is everywhere, why is the word *digital* even needed anymore? Digital savvy will become part of how we define talent.

Talent selection, training, career development, and ongoing community will continue to be very important—but in a full-spectrum future where the human and computer resources will be blended and inseparable. For talent selection, for example, new media will allow much more meaningful connection during the recruiting process. It will be possible to share real-life experiences of the job with a candidate to entice, test the fit, and ensure that the person is a good match to the job. It will be easier to make the right hire the first time.

Video Gaming to Learn

Training and employee development are critical to the human resources function, and there are already profound signals of disruptive change from traditional HR training. Here are two signals:

First, on August 10, 2018, a Sea-Tac Airport maintenance worker stole an aircraft and took off for an amazing joy ride. The plane was a Bombardier Dash 8 Q400. It had no locking system because it was so difficult to operate that nobody imagined it could be flown by anyone other than a trained pilot.

The thief flew this complicated aircraft around Puget Sound, circling with an impressive series of aerial acrobatics, including barrel rolls that only the most elite pilots are able to perform. While the plane was stunt flying, the control tower asked if the thief needed help in landing the aircraft. He said something like "Nah, I'm good." They asked him if he was a pilot. "No." They asked him how he'd learned to fly, and his shrugging answer was this: "I've played some video games."

The full story will never come out, since after his circus performance the unauthorized and uncredentialled pilot seemed to intentionally crash the plane and kill himself. The mystery was how he learned to fly that very complicated airplane with cockpit controls that look ridiculously complex. The answer was this: the airplane thief learned how to fly a real plane by playing a virtual reality video game that is a remarkably accurate rendering of the actual cockpit and controls.

Playing this video game is very much like flying the real aircraft, as the thief proved. Flight simulators have been used for pilot training for years, but now they are being built into everyday video games that can be played by anyone—not just pilots in training. What we call video gaming today is sneaking under the tent into the world of learning.

Another signal: My colleague Dylan Hendricks is from Canada but now lives in Texas. He was invited by his brother-in-law to go trap shooting. In this sport, participants use a real shotgun to shoot small "clay pigeons" that are projected up into the air by a spring-loaded launcher. Dylan had very little experience shooting any kind of gun, and he had never shot a real shotgun. He is in fact antigun, true to his Canadian roots. Out on the range, he was trying to figure out how not to embarrass himself in front of his brother-in-law and the expert Texas shooters all around him.

"Pull," he said, and the clay pigeon flew up and he—to his great surprise—shot it right out of the air!

He continued on, scoring at a very good rate and convincing his family that he had been lying about his lack of shooting skills. They were convinced he was secretly an expert marksman falsely claiming to be a novice. His family was confused and not amused.

Dylan himself was stunned, until he remembered how he had played a virtual reality game called Duck Hunt. By playing that game, he had unconsciously learned that skill—even though he used game controllers and not a pretend gun. The muscle memory of the game apparently simulates very accurately the physics of how to line up the sights on a target and anticipate movement.

As superminds emerge, humans will learn how to combine their skills with those of advanced digital tools and media. Human skills and computer augmentation will blend in powerful new ways that are already apparent in the world of gaming.

Few people are noticing that video gaming is transforming from entertainment to learning media. Playing video games requires both human and computing resources, but the experience of learning is a much more elegant mix than what most of us ever experienced in schools.

Institute for the Future's Jane McGonigal, one of the world's leading designers of socially constructive games, defines gaming as "emotionally laden attention." I find it fascinating that this is the same definition used to define a good story. A good game is a good story where you can actually be *in* the story, not just read the story.

Today's video gaming interfaces are often at least 10 times better than anything we have in offices. These vivid interfaces, combined with powerful storytelling, will create the powerful and unprecedented learning environment I am forecasting. The video gaming industry has prototyped—often in very distasteful ways—a new medium for learning and training.

I know that my forecast that video gaming will become a powerful learning medium is hard to imagine for many parents, especially those who categorize today's video games as a danger to be managed. I agree with the very understandable parental assessment that many of today's video games are too sexual and too violent. The challenge for us today is to look beyond distasteful video gaming content to the medium of gaming to the potential for gaming as a way of teaching a range of socially constructive content.

And, in corporate environments, who will teach through this new medium? People from the human resources function, the folks we have come to call HR. Today's HR practitioners will be called on to become experts in this new teaching and learning medium. If they do not, some other function will step up to replace them. This is a chance to reimagine and up the stakes for HR as we know it today.

My forecast is that, in the future, most human resources practitioners will be gamers. I don't necessarily mean that they will be experts in playing today's video games, but rather that they will be experts in the medium of immersive learning through digital and in-person experiences.

Orson Scott Card describes the value of gaming and immersive learning this way:

The essence of training is to allow error without consequence.[4]

In *Ender's Game*, gaming is used as a powerful learning medium to prepare Earth for an attack from alien beings. The thesis of the book and the movie, as I introduced in Chapter 6, is that the most gifted young gamers with the most fluid minds will be best prepared to meet the challenges of war. The kids learned to be warriors through playing video games so complicated that their elders weren't able to play them.

To get ready for the future, the HR function should be recruiting gamers today.

Think HCR, Not Just HR

The blending of humans and computers will present many more challenges and opportunities that are invading the traditional HR space. Signals are here already, and they are ready to scale. They've been a long time coming.

Just after 9/11, I was asked to do a forecast on the future of fun at Walt Disney World in Orlando. In that tense mood after 9/11, parents were understandably concerned about safety while kids wanted a play-oriented experience where they could be scared in a safe way. The Magic Kingdom was a place to go to escape the trauma of the everyday world where terrorism loomed.

This was the same period when Walt Disney World was testing what became the Magic Band that guests wear throughout the park to keep track of their location and guide them to the shortest lines—as well as making it easy to pay and move around. I introduced my experience with the early prototype called Pal Mickey in Chapter 7, and this experience yielded an important lesson about learning for me. I wore Pal Mickey hooked on my belt, and it guided me through the park.

My Pal Mickey prototype stopped working while I was out in the park one day, and I stumbled upon an important aspect of what makes Walt Disney World so magical—a lesson that combines human and computer capabilities. I brought my malfunctioning Pal Mickey to one of the cast members (the term that Walt Disney World uses to describe employees), and she said no problem, she would give me a new one. I was disappointed, however, that I had to give up *my* Pal Mickey. I asked if she could heal my Pal Mickey, rather than give me a new one.

She paused for just a moment but then said something like "Oh, I think I saw a wizard passing by just a moment ago. Let me see what he can do." And she slipped behind a curtain. She returned bursting with enthusiasm. "Your Pal Mickey has been healed!" I'm quite sure that she gave me a new Pal Mickey that worked, but she did it so gracefully and with such charm that I happily went on my way.

Walt Disney World is well known for animatronics, where they create realistic models of presidents and other famous people. More subtly, Walt Disney World has also mastered the art of blending human and machine resources. Their "cast members" use a wide range of digital tools while still maintaining a very human touch to create magical experiences for the guests. All human resources organizations in the future will need that same skill. I haven't seen an HR organization yet that comes close to what I've experienced at Walt Disney World.

Pal Mickey evolved into the Magic Band. This elegant wristband doesn't feel like a computer, but Walt Disney World is now a giant computer-enhanced world where kids can be safely scared. But it isn't *just* a computer; it is a magical mix of human and computer resources. The cast members are now augmented in ways that don't automate but do amplify the experience. Powerful computing power is delivered in a very human way.

We see even more dramatic signals of human-computer augmentation in health, health care, and well-being. I met the computer scientist Larry Smarr years ago because of his work with supercomputers and visualization. As I got to know him personally, I realized that he was applying his considerable computer science expertise to visualize and monitor his health and peer at his own organs—and he had been doing it for years.

Think *human* resources (I really like the term *human resources*; I really don't like the term *HR*) in concert with *computing*, *media*, and *robotics* tools. Human-computing resources will prioritize continuous learning for workers through gameful engagement pedagogies as it becomes the most powerful learning medium in history.

HR Has Yet Another Chance to Transform

I fear that some of today's HR leaders and practitioners may not be ready or willing for this transformation. In my career, the human resources function has had several opportunities to embrace technology and develop a new human-centered lens to help scale technology across organizations in humanistic ways. Recall these new technologies of old:

- Teleconferencing
- Groupware
- Office automation
- Artificial intelligence

In each case, the human resources function had the opportunity to lead the way and embrace an emerging technology while helping others figure out how to use it well. In each case, the HR function and HR people stepped away instead of stepping up. The information technology (IT) people usually took the lead, but many of them had very limited personal and organizational skills. HR stayed on the sidelines—except in a few very interesting cases.

Now, the human resources function has another opportunity to embrace new technology and add human and organizational spice to the mix. I hope they will take on the opportunity this time. Human resources can lead the way.

They will only have a short window of opportunity to learn and engage with the next wave of computing, communications, and gaming. The HR people may not be invited to the table by the technologists and top executives. My hope is that human resources people will call the meeting, rather than wait until they are invited.

If they don't get invited or don't act, however, the human resources function is likely to go down a declining HR path of being outsourced and undervalued. I believe that we will have a much better and more productive future if technology and human resources are mixed. I also believe that it will be easier to teach human resources people about technology than it would be to teach technology people about human resources. This was not true when the technology was more difficult to use, but it is now, and it will be even more true in the future.

The new HCR leaders will have the potential to reinvent their function as they reinvent organizations as we know them—and reinvent themselves. Human and computer resources will blend in new ways as the line between human and machine gets increasingly blurred. Collective intelligence— humans working together, augmented by machines—will be required to thrive. These are the "superminds"[5] that Thomas W. Malone talks about. This is exactly where the HR profession should be focused. Humans alone certainly won't be enough, but neither will computers. HR professionals are in the best position to help answer the fundamental questions of what humans can do best and what computers can do best.

HR leaders will need full-spectrum thinking, and they will need to teach full-spectrum thinking to others. Full-spectrum thinking will be necessary for both work and private life in the future.

To thrive, leaders will need new full-spectrum thinking capabilities and skills to make good use of the emerging tools and media. Companies, non-profits, and government agencies will be required by the market to offer a wide spectrum of working arrangements for making a living while having a life.

Ellen Galinsky founded the Families and Work Institute and was one of the early explorers of what came to be called work-life balance. After years of studying the trade-offs of work vs. private life, she embarked on a search for a better word than *balance*, since it seemed for many people that balance was an impossible goal. Her conclusion after months of searching and pondering was that the word *navigation* was a much better fit. As with any other kind of navigation, there are fixed and fluid variables—and a lot of choices. Increasingly, human resource professionals will need to be whole-life professionals—and whole life will include digital augmentation possibilities.

The networking technologies I described in Chapter 5 will make it much easier to work anytime anyplace, although this kind of distributed work will require social and individual discipline, as well as technological support. I call this the ability to be there without being there.[6] Silicon Valley is now leading the way on distributed work, a path made urgent by the ridiculous housing prices in the Bay Area. Fortunately, the tools for distributed work will get even more advanced over the next decade.

Recall the AG Lafley story from Chapter 1 where he told P&G alumni that P&G could no longer offer lifelong employment but could offer lifelong *employability*. That's just what is needed in the increasingly flexible gig economy with many micromarkets and porous boundaries between companies.

When I spoke to a group of Silicon Valley CEOs recently, they all shared a concern that career paths in this future world that is already here in Silicon Valley will get increasingly harder to navigate and also make it harder for people to measure their own progress. In the increasingly fluid organizational world (Silicon Valley is an extreme example), the traditional ways of tracking career progress, such as salary raises, new titles, and clearly marked career ladders, just don't make as much sense. Often in Silicon Valley and especially with younger workers, experiences are valued more than money or titles.

The HCR function will be able to identify a range of options for work and private life. Then, HCR can help identify the options and guide choice making to provide value for the firm and for the worker.

As I was writing this book, Institute for the Future hired its first cyborg anthropologist, Amber Case.[7] She studies symbiotic interactions between humans and machines, as well as how our values and culture are increasingly shaped by new technologies. HCR professionals will need the skills and mentality of cyborg anthropology.

Every human will have the potential to be augmented by machines in some ways. The art and science of this augmentation will be the focus on the reimagined human resources professional. The more intelligent computers become, the more humans will value other humans. The more digital we become, the more we will value human interaction. The more alike computers and people become, the more we will value the differences.

I asked several chief human resources officers to review drafts of this chapter. Vicki Lostetter is CHRO at WestRock, one of the world's largest paper companies. She had worked previously as a human resources leader at Coca-Cola and Microsoft. Here is her thoughtful reaction:

> The role of human resources will be to prepare our organizations for this change and to continue to keep the right "touch" in the organization— or keep the "human" in our work environment as we blend human and computing for better outcomes. One last plug—inspire human resources leaders to have the courage to learn more and take on this brave new world that is emerging—be the role models of try, fail fast, cheap and try again. Be in front.[8]

It is already too late for any human resources professional to work without a deep understanding of digital media. How can technology empower and enhance human skills? Human resources professionals need very good answers to this question. It is a great time for the human resources function to leapfrog into human-computing resources (HCR). HCR has the potential to transform individuals, organizations, and society. The stakes are high for human resources.

CHAPTER 10

Broader Spectrums of Diversity

New Inclusive Paths to Innovation

ALAN TURING, A BRITISH HERO IN WORLD WAR II, WAS labeled gay by the British government and persecuted brutally. Even while he was being so painfully categorized, Turing was saving England by inventing the ultimate categorization machine, what we now call the computer. Being categorized was dangerous for Turing, and it still is dangerous for many people today.

As comedian, actor, and writer Hannah Gadsby says in her powerful 2018 performance of *Nanette*, "It is dangerous to be different."[1]

The movie *The Imitation Game* is about Turing and how he cracked German codes during World War II using his early computer. He was portrayed as an unlikely genius who seemed both weird and annoying to many people around him. The movie asked viewers to ponder this:

Sometimes it is the people no one can imagine anything of who do the things no one can imagine.[2]

The cruel and biting irony of Alan Turing, however, set the stage for much better things to come as computing gradually evolves from binary forced choices to helping us understand the full spectrum of human identities and powers.

Turing's computer reduced everything to zeros and ones. In the rigid either/or world that Turing created, we have benefited from new power to categorize, organize, and compute. But people have also suffered under the severe limitations of overcategorizing.

Gender as a Spectrum

When my colleague Gabe Cervantes joined the Institute to work with me on this book, the first task I asked him to do was create a new account on Facebook and see how many gender options he could find. To our surprise in the summer of 2018, he was offered 59 different gender options, including agender, bigender, cisgender, gender nonconforming, gender questioning, pangender, a variety of transgender options, and two-spirit. How many different categories does it take before we start to think of gender as a spectrum of possibilities?

On the other hand, some people may not self-identify as on a spectrum. Some may want to be categorized. Some may want to create their own categories—or use no categories at all. Again, categorizing yourself is very different from categorizing others. This book is mostly about categorizing others.

Full-spectrum thinking about gender goes deep into history and biology, as highlighted by Alexandra Kralick in a 2018 *Discover* article:

> An increasing recognition of this complexity by researchers and the public has affirmed that gender sits on a spectrum: People are more and more willing to acknowledge the reality of nonbinary and transgender identities, and to support those who courageously fight for their rights in everything from all-gender bathrooms to anti-gender-discrimination laws. But underlying all of this is the perception that no matter the gender a person identifies as, they have an underlying sex they were born with. This represents a fundamental misunderstanding about the nature of biological sex. Science keeps showing us that sex also doesn't fit in a binary, whether it be determined by genitals, chromosomes, hormones, or bones.[3]

The fact that "sex also doesn't fit in a binary" is a very important understanding that is based in science—not in culture or religious belief. "Gender sits on a spectrum," yet we continue to talk about it as if it were a predetermined either/or, or an either/or choice. That gender is by definition a spectrum is the starting point for a very different kind of conversation.

If you assume a rational and humanistic world, it is reasonable to expect a broader spectrum for gender identities in the future—not just two forced-choice categories. Leaders will need flexibility, fluidity, and empathy to have any sense of how to engage constructively. Quick judgments will risk mistakes and offense. In the world of gender, we are clearly moving from static to fluid, with a range of options that is yet to be determined—and may never be fully determined. And gender is just one of many kinds of diversity.

Diversity will become more important even as it becomes more difficult to categorize. Thinking across the age spectrum will be particularly important—especially the category currently called "retirees," which is increasingly made up of people who either don't want to or can't afford to retire. Chip Conley was the founder of a very successful boutique hotel chain, and he ran it until he was 50 years old. Then, in his early fifties, he was recruited by Airbnb to be a modern corporate elder, a "mentern"—part mentor, part intern.

Aging as a Spectrum

Chip Conley tells his story in an inspiring book on full-spectrum thinking about age called *Wisdom@Work: The Making of a Modern Elder*. He points out that only 8 percent of companies have a diversity and inclusion strategy that includes age (what Conley calls a longevity strategy). He sees this as an opportunity for innovation and growth:

> When it comes to the fact that an extra decade of living means workers staying on their jobs longer and customers spending money on midlife purchases later in life, what innovations can you offer to older employees or customers that set you apart from your competitors?...The bottom line is: your longevity strategy isn't just a feel-good measure; it's good business strategy.[4]

In November of 2018, Conley opened The Modern Elder Academy in El Pescadero, Mexico, where he offers one-week programs and extended stays. This program teaches that contributions from the modern elder will be just as important as contributions from the digital natives. The Modern Elder Academy is thinking more broadly about the age spectrum and the value that elders can provide. Nellie Bowles reported in *The New York Times*:

> There was a growing sense of empowerment and camaraderie—almost rebellion. Mr. Conley talked about reclaiming the term *elder* like the gay community has reclaimed *queer*.
>
> "The social narrative is basically, midlife is a crisis and after a crisis you have decrepitude," Mr. Conley said. "But you actually are much happier in your 60s and 70s, so why aren't we preparing for that?"[5]

Approaching the American football Super Bowl in 2019, I heard 41-year-old New England Patriots quarterback Tom Brady interviewed about how he can continue playing at such an advanced age for professional football players. His answer was that at this stage in his career, he has seen everything. The game just gets easier for him with more experience, he said.

Full-spectrum thinking will aid in the search for clarity and reveal the limitations of our assumptions about diversity. We're all learning how to play the wisdom game. In my experience, the game does get easier the longer we play it. Tom Brady's goal is to play professional football until he is 45. I'm a writer and my goal is to continue writing as long as I'm having fun and able to write books that people will use.

Young people seem much more accepting of diversity than older people. Among younger generations, diversity is sometimes a badge. Recently, I heard someone say this proudly: "I am biracial + queer + gender nonbinary + working class + first generation to go to college." Categories won't go away in the future, but they will become more fluid and cross-spectrum. Even individual people will become what my colleague Anthony Weeks calls "an identity of multiples." Another colleague, Rachel Hatch, refers to the "three business card life" as a way to describe people making a living across a spectrum of work options rather than a single profession.

Many younger people do not want to be forced to choose between being queer vs. a person of color, a woman vs. a person who is working class, an immigrant vs. a person with a college education. All identities are important and vital, they say. Having to choose can be perceived as an imposition by some power structure. "I don't want to choose! I want an identity that is complex and intersectional!" they say. "I don't want to be categorized, particularly by categories that others slap on me."

Forming alliances across spectrums of diversity means that on some issues, allies will agree, but on others, they will be in opposition. How will we navigate the complexity of shifting allegiances in a world where we are sometimes best friends, and other times ideological foes?

Even within designated communities such as the queer/LGBT community, Latinx community, or African American community, there are differences around a variety of issues. How will we think of community in such a context, especially when community may be in itself an unstable category?

People with Disabilities as a Spectrum

In 2007, I led a custom forecast with distinguished fellow Kathi Vian from IFTF on external future forces likely to disrupt people with disabilities, thinking 10 years ahead. This research was supported by United Cerebral Palsy and a group of private foundations,[6] and our forecast proved very accurate. It yielded a structure that I have built upon for this chapter as we think ahead now to 2030.

My first lesson from that project was what is called the people-first principle. If we follow this principle, instead of labeling a person as "disabled," we will say "a person with a disability." This principle suggests that we always start with the person, not the label. The person-first principle is in fact a kind of broad-spectrum thinking, rather than starting from a single category or label. Categories of action and thought don't function as well for a person with disabilities, so it is easier for them to think outside boxes and norms to find a way that works for them.

In San Francisco, the Board of Supervisors is applying the person-first principle to the criminal justice system. Supervisor Matt Haney said, "We don't want people to be forever labeled for the worst things they have done… we want them ultimately to become contributing citizens, and referring to them as felons is like a scarlet letter that they can never get away from."[7]

The possibilities will be shifting for those who are different. Strong currents of change—both promising and threatening—will change the global landscape in a way that will reshape the very idea of diversity and inclusion.

People will reach to extend their capacity, not just economically but physically, mentally, and socially as well. New technologies will help people reimagine what human bodies and minds can do. People will be able to turn their own bodies into laboratories for innovation and creativity. Imagining ourselves in this future, perhaps everyone will see themself as a person with disabilities in search of augmentation to improve.

Spectrum inclusion begins with ourselves, and it will include the diverse capabilities we will be able to develop in a creative blending of human, computing, and robotic potential. We are all destined to be cyborgs, and that will be a good thing overall.

Diversity Correlates with Innovation

In his book *The Diversity [Bonus]*, University of Michigan and Santa Fe Institute scholar Scott Page argues that carefully crafted diverse teams are better able to solve complex problems. He argues that a careful mixing of both cognitive and identity diversity leads to better outcomes. Drawing from a range of real-world case studies, Page argues that there is an inherent bonus (and added monetary incentive) for diverse teams in corporate settings. Page's data shows that diversity is directly correlated with innovation. I find his conclusion particularly compelling, since he is not a social activist; he's a big data analytics expert.

In his earlier book called *The Difference*, Scott Page summarized his conclusion as follows: "Almost by definition, breakthroughs require serendipity. That serendipity arises from diverse preparedness. It derives from someone noticing and knowing how to interpret strange phenomena."[8] Spectrum inclusion is a foundational ingredient in a recipe for innovation.

The value and values of diversity must be seeded, nurtured, and grown before they can be harvested, however. #VanguardSTEM is a website where women of color in the STEM fields offer live discussions around topics like "research interests, wisdom, advice, tips, tricks and commentary on current events." #VanguardSTEM is seeding a community for women of color so that they can learn from and educate each other within the largely white-male-dominated field of STEM research.[9] The guiding principle is to create conversations between emerging and established women of color in STEM in a safe space where they can celebrate and affirm their identities and STEM interests. Moderated by founder and host Dr. Jedidah Isler, viewers share questions and input via social media in real time.

The value and values of diversity play out on a daily basis during meetings of all kinds. My colleague Anthony Weeks is a public listener who records and draws while he listens to group conversations. He creates beautiful works of business art that summarize group conversations. He is an expert practitioner of the art of listening, an art that we all must learn in order to listen across spectrums of diversity. Here's how he describes his art:

> Listening is hard—and humbling. We find out what we don't know. We find out who we are. We find out what it means to live in that space on the edge, where the only bridge to our humanity is the intersection between our own ability to listen and the voices who are clamoring to be heard. How can I give of myself while not giving myself away? There's a difference. We need not agree, at first. We need only agree that our own story is not the only one. Our stories contain multitudes, if we are willing to listen.[10]

Anthony Weeks is both a graphic recorder and a documentary film maker. He listens for stories. The stories of spectrum diversity will be increasingly rich and powerful.

I like to imagine futures thinking as the art of listening for the future. The full-spectrum future will be made up of many different voices and sounds, both familiar and foreign.

My Forecast for Spectrum Diversity

Here is my forecast for spectrum diversity and inclusion, looking out over the next decade:[11]

A wide spectrum of *individual* augmented people and superminds will be commonplace in *organizations* and *society*. We will have an ever-expanding view of human capacity. In my book *The New Leadership Literacies*,

I discussed the leadership literacy of creating and sustaining positive energy.[12] My forecast at the end of that book in 2017 was that successful future leaders will all be body hackers in the sense that they will aggressively alter their own bodies to increase performance and healthy living. Reactive health care will yield to proactive well-being and superempowered performance.

Lightweight distributed infrastructures will attract greater *organizational* diversity across *societies*. The growth of flexible systems for supporting life on the planet will scale in ways that make spectrum inclusion operational. In Chapter 5, I described the emerging world of distributed-authority networks, and this world will make very powerful resources available to local groups and individuals. In this world, very small groups will be able to do very large things—for good and for evil.

The group economy will make it more attractive for *individuals*, *organizations*, and *societies* to be inclusive. Economies of scale and economies of organization will favor diversity and responsiveness. As coordination costs drop because of digital connectivity, new groups will emerge as an economic layer between institutions and individuals—just as Uber and Lyft are a layer between drivers and riders. This emerging group economy will be a kind of economy of scale, but it will also be an economy of organization. Groups will be what they can organize, and their tools for organizing will be dramatically better. Group economies will have the motivation and flexibility to celebrate diversity and support differences in ways that traditional institutions rarely did.

New tools, new networks, and the true digital natives will broaden how people think about varied lifestyles and ways of living. Technology is on a trajectory from computing to communications to sensing our environment and our bodies. Sense-making will be a new frontier as environments become aware and responsive to those who occupy them. There is potential here for assistance to come in the form of digital augmentation—not automation.

Nationalism and globalism will mix across *societies*. The politics and economics of global diversity and inclusiveness will continue to be a source of tension and strife. Diverse people with diverse identities will be targeted as markets, connected with lightweight infrastructures, and committed to growing their own distinctive identities. In particular, people from less prosperous portions of the world will stake claim to new global identities using new digital tools for organizing.

Sustainably diverse *organizations* and *societies* will be scalable and profitable. There will be a pressing imperative to redesign our communities to support healthy living. Cities and local communities will take the lead in addressing the big global dilemmas of sustainability. Pollution, climate disruption, and population growth dilemmas will continue to threaten in ominous ways. Meanwhile, companies large and small will figure out ways to flip these dilemmas into profitable opportunities to do good while doing well.

When I was in divinity school, diversity was all about equity and social justice. Now and in the future, diversity will *also* be about innovation. Social justice issues are even more urgent than they were in the 1960s, but now there are strong big data analytics arguments from Scott Page and others to document the innovation bonus that diversity of all kinds will provide.

The preferred talent profile will be a provocative mix of grit with grace, strength with humility, and cognitive diversity that correlates with innovation. Diversity will no longer be about social equity alone. Diversity and spectrum inclusion will lead to innovation—but not in straight lines, with quotas, or by predesignated categories.

For individuals, the options and awareness are opening new opportunities. For organizations and societies, there are new responsibilities—but now the advantages are obvious.

CHAPTER 11

Broader Spectrums of Meaning

A New Game of Hope

WHEN MY DAD DIED, MY MOM SAID "I HAVE FAITH. I don't know what I believe, but I have faith."

They had been married for 60 years, and my Mom didn't feel any certainty after my Dad's death. Still, she felt something that she called faith.

Faith arises out of limited human understanding, but it nudges people toward expansive full-spectrum thinking about life possibilities. Faith is related to clarity. Faith kindles hope.

But faith is not the same as certainty; faith is not an answer. Faith includes questions—usually lots of questions. Faith is at least a touch fuzzy. Faith is inherently future oriented.

Faith grows out of a learning mindset. Faith allows you to navigate your way through things you don't have all figured out. Faith helps you make your way through fear. Faith is grounded in a sense of humility and openness to learning in an uncertain future. Faith implies a full-spectrum mindset.

Faith lives in the space between insight and action, the same space where strategy lives. That's why it's called a "leap" of faith. Introducing a new strategy is a leap of faith. As with strategy, faith requires directional clarity but great flexibility in how faith is lived out. Faith shapes the kind of future we are able to imagine.

I believe we are moving toward new spectrums of meaning-making that will help us increase clarity and decrease certainty. Faith in the future will be even more important than it has been in the past. Faith seeds hope.

Faith: Clarity—but Not Certainty

In the long run, the scrambled future will reward clarity—but punish certainty. Certainty will be too brittle and inflexible for the scrambled future we will be facing. Spectrum thinking will help us understand the many forms of meaning and meaning-making. Categorical thinking will leave us mired in false certainty.

Faith promises clarity but doesn't tell you what to do. Faith is directional, but not explicit. Faith informs individual choice, but the higher ground of faith is trust and confidence.

Many people confuse faith with certainty. To inspire faith in someone is to empower them, but faith is humble. Certainty is arrogant.

Certainty, unlike faith, is locked in hindsight. As theologian Paul Tillich said, the opposite of faith is not doubt; the opposite of faith is certainty. I first read Tillich when I was in divinity school, and his writing helped me understand the value of faith and the dangers of rigid belief.

Certainty is rigid categorization. Certainty is freezing the truth. "True believers"[1] categorize obsessively. They want to know whether others are in or out—whether or not they are true believers. And, with true believers, there are usually only two choices. The ultimate power play is to claim that god is on your side—and not on the other side.

For people of Christian faith, foresight is shaped and informed by what has become known as the Wesleyan Quadrilateral: scripture, tradition, reason, and experience. Faith helps us imagine a better future.

When Institute for the Future did a custom forecast for the Consortium of Endowed Episcopal Parishes of the Episcopal Church in 2007, I learned about the Anglican notion of "discerning questions." A discerning question cannot be answered with a yes or no. Discerning questions are part of a fitness program for developing faith and clarity. Discerning questions challenge certainty and cultivate clarity. Foresight often provokes powerful discerning questions.

Meaning-Making as a Spectrum

My favorite definition of religion is "meaning–making." Traditional religion is yielding to distributed-authority meaning-making in ways that I find very exciting and mind opening. At Harvard Divinity School, for example, a very unusual project is under way to map the spectrums of meaning-making outside organized religion, at the edges of the sacred and the secular. As the poet-songwriter Leonard Cohen said in his song "Anthem": "There is a crack, a crack in everything. That's how the light gets in."

Casper ter Kuile, Angie Thurston, and Sue Phillips are the core team for this exploration, which has already yielded remarkable insight: "Our expression of religious life is dying. We need containers that give spiritual permission and show people how to be together, containers that allow people to derive meaning. Containers that are safe enough to allow people to try something."[2] Fear—especially categorical fear of others—is a shallow container for meaning. The team is exploring broader spectrums of meaning-making. They want to understand the new models for meaning-making, how they are expressed, and how they could be turned into meaningful habits or rituals of faith on a larger scale.

After studying these new spiritual movements for the last few years, they have concluded that we are in a "very juicy moment in history," where meaning-making is a growth industry.[3] Are we approaching an inflection point? They think we are, and I would like to believe that we are.

In 1995, I led a project probe at Institute for the Future called Good Company: What's the Meaning of Work? I had just finished a book with novelist Rob Swigart called *Upsizing the Individual in the Downsized Organization*[4] that convinced us that

> life after downsizing often means fewer managers managing more people with more cultural diversity and more geographic separation, but less (or no) corporate loyalty. For the survivors as well as the dispossessed, this left a void of meaning at the core of many organizations.[5]

The mood in 1995, in the wake of the disappointments of the reengineering movement, seemed ripe to me for strong interest in meaning-making. Our report contained many examples of meaning-making innovations that were under way and looked promising. When we reviewed those efforts in 2019, most of them had ended. The quest for meaning is persistent, but the successful efforts to make meaning over time are rare.

The core research question for the Harvard Divinity School team is this:

How can we retrieve the ancient wisdom,
without the constraints?

In a beautiful, substantive, and accessible report they called "How We Gather," the Harvard team identified a wide range of valid spiritual practices that are not part of any organized religion. Six core meaning-making themes were recurring across a wide spectrum of the activities they studied:

- Community: valuing and fostering deep relationships that center on service to others. Communities focused on exercise and health are particularly popular signals right now. Creating new communities is often more powerful than simply joining existing communities. Communities in the future will be increasingly virtual, but the more virtual we become, the more we will value in-person experiences.[6]

- Personal transformation: making a conscious and dedicated effort to develop one's own body, mind, and spirit. Again, exercise and health are very motivational, and people are willing to pay for these experiences. The emergence of cheap and connected body sensors will help people make healthy choices.

- Social transformation: pursuing justice and beauty in the world through the creation of networks for good. The looming societal challenges of today—particularly the asset gap and global climate disruption—are particularly powerful motivators. Global connectivity will make social transformations across geographies more likely.

- Purpose finding: clarifying, articulating, and acting on one's personal mission in life. Hope is the key variable here.

- Creativity: allowing time and space to activate the imagination and engage in play. Gameful engagement will grow in popularity as digital interfaces become increasingly robust.

- Accountability: holding oneself and others responsible for working toward defined goals. Tracking and sensing systems will make it easier to account for transactions and communications, sometimes without any central authority.

The rituals and practices of spiritual life are clearly changing, but the direction of change is not yet apparent. The new experiences are difficult to categorize. While habits are automatic and mindless, rituals are iterative but mindful. Rituals are a condensed code of meaning, and repeating the code reinforces the meaning. My wife and I, for example, say "I love you" to each other at least a few times each day. Why do we say it again and again to each other every day even though we already said it several times yesterday and the day before that?

Information Is Not the Same as Meaning

The sociologist of religion Robert Bellah explains the very human need for iterations of meaning in order to keep the connection alive. These ritual habits become even more important, he says, in a world where we often have access to more information, but less meaning:

> Meaning is dependent on the condensed code. We might begin to understand that though the word is frequently used, meaning is not nearly as central to our present concerns as information. After all, meaning doesn't tell us something new, it seems just to be saying the same old thing, though in a deeper understanding it makes sense of the new. Meaning is iterative, not cumulative...the request was not for information but for the reiteration of meaning.[7]

Bellah goes on in this article to tell the story of one of his graduate students, a pastor in an urban California congregation. The pastor/student was asked to the home of a dying woman who had been in a coma near death for many days. After a conversation with the woman's daughter, the pastor suggested that they go into the room of the dying woman and pray with her. The daughter resisted taking the pastor into the room with her mother, since the mother had been in a coma for so long, but the pastor insisted. The pastor started with the Lord's Prayer and was barely into "Our Father who art in heaven" when the dying woman in a coma woke up and joined in the prayer. She stayed out of the coma for several days and had significant conversations with her daughter before she died.

Bellah's takeaway: "The request was not for information but for reiteration of meaning." Codes of meaning like the Lord's Prayer or "I love you" embody meaning in an active way so we can all carry on the story in which we are playing a part. The core story could be the same for a child or an elder, but as we age, more meaning gets rolled in with the iterations—so the story lives and grows in importance.

Our challenge in 2020 (Bellah's essay was written in 2001) is that many of the ancient codes of meaning no longer carry the same sense of meaning for many—maybe most—people. Certainly, an unbundling and remixing of our stories of meaning is under way. Many of the ancient stories just don't have the same zest and vitality that they once did.

In a full-spectrum world, meaningful iterative habits will be critical to keeping our meaningful stories alive. How might new digital tools and networks help keep ancient stories of meaning alive and engaging? Virtual churches are an obvious possibility and there are signals today, but I am more interested in ways to do gameful engagement in the meaning-making space. I don't know what that looks like, but I do see some hints.

The Harvard team is studying attempts to revive ancient meaning-making and sorting the current signals into pursuits of (1) belonging, to relieve isolation and help people connect, and (2) becoming, a meaning-making void for many people who are asking basic human questions like Who am I? Why am I here? These questions call for full-spectrum thinking about meaning.

Even with the massive boom in information available, people are still seeking meaning—maybe more so than ever. Rituals and habits can be a condensed code for meaning, but only if the stories are alive in the minds of believers. In a world exploding with uncertainty, certainty about something—anything—can seem a relief. Certainty bestows power, but it also invites abuse.

The culture of sexual abuse in the Catholic Church, for example, was clearly linked to both faith and power. God is, for many believers, the ultimate power. Those who claim or are perceived to have a special relationship with god are sometimes granted unusual power. Abuse can be an unfortunate by-product.

When I was in divinity school, I was introduced to the notion of pastoral psychology—a combination of psychology and theology. I was intrigued at first but became sobered by the delicate balance of power when a psychologist claims an additional right of way by implying some sort of divine access. While I could see the potential to benefit from a mix of psychology and religion, the dangers were looming. Psychology is imposing enough, but holy psychology was too much for me. I drifted away from churches, in spite of having earned the academic degree necessary to be ordained. I felt the need to broaden my spectrum of inquiry, and I just found the church too constraining.

Human–machine symbiosis could add an additional dimension of meaning. How might hybrids of machines and humans develop new experiences of meaning-making?

We all have to find meaning for ourselves, and sometimes this gets harder when we age. Chip Conley, the hospitality innovator now focused on corporate elders who I discussed in Chapter 10, talks about how he hid his gray hair until his fifties. Then, he grew Hemingway-like gray whiskers. When he saw an old friend, he asked her, "Does this beard age me?" She said, "No, darling, it sages you."

Age gives us license to play the wisdom game, and the game gets more serious the more we age. The wisdom of age gives us something we can offer in cross-generational exchanges. The digital natives grew up digital, but age and experience give digital immigrants (all of us older than 25 in 2020) a different and possibly useful sense of what is important.

My Forecast for Meaning and Well-Being

Larry Smarr may know more about the workings of his own body than any other person on Earth. He is an extreme example of what has come to be called the "quantified self movement" that began in Silicon Valley almost a decade ago and accelerated the popularity of body sensors to monitor our steps and body functions to help us make healthier choices. His goal is for every person to become the CEO of their own body.[8]

Today, Larry Smarr is a highly unusual human being working with very special computing resources to understand and manage his own body. Ten years from now, normal people will have access to similar resources for well-being. Computing will augment human talents, not just automate routine tasks. And the human resources function will include a strong focus on health and well-being. Larry Smarr is a signal that hints at how we will all have new full-spectrum views of our own bodies and how we can make healthier choices.

About 10 years ago, I helped Humana create an innovation board to explore the future of health and well-being. As part of this effort, IFTF worked with Humana and Gallup to create a map of the elements of health and well-being—thinking 10 years ahead. So often in the US, "health care" really means "sick care," and we don't devote much time at all to developing all aspects of health and well-being. I believe that meaning-making implies successful engagement in all of these aspects of life and living:

- Physical
- Mindful
- Interpersonal
- Societal
- Financial
- In-work
- Spiritual[9]

In *The New Leadership Literacies*, I built on this well-being model to make a forecast of how the best leaders will develop their own well-being in the future, thinking 10 years ahead. Each of these combinations of leadership and skills fits into a larger spectrum of meaning-making. I believe that increasingly over the next decade, meaning will be connected to physical and mental health and well-being. Four elements of well-being will be particularly important for new spectrums of meaning:

A body-hacking mindset will be linked with meaning-making. Continuous external and internal body sensing will help us make better health choices. Physical well-being is basic to meaning-making. If we aren't physically healthy, it is much harder to find meaning.

When I was in divinity school, "biofeedback" was the new trendy California thing to aid in meditation and what we would now call mindfulness. The real challenge with biofeedback is knowing what the best pattern is for us. Having someone else who monitors our patterns can be very helpful.

Over the next decade, sensors will be very cheap, very small, and very connected. An increasing proportion of those sensors will be inside our bodies. Health care won't just be outside in; it will be inside out. Already, at most of my speaking engagements, half of the participants wear body sensors of some sort to help them track their fitness and make healthy choices. Ten years from now, everyone who wants one will wear a body sensor, and half of us will have some sort of imbedded body sensor. All of us will be cyborgs.

Self-knowledge of your own brain will make it easier to understand the process of meaning-making. Over the next decade, neuroscience will become practical. As we understand our brains and our minds better, we will be able to understand better how meaning is derived. Our brains like to put new things in old boxes. Next-generation tools, networks, and neuroscience understanding will help us teach our brains the new tricks of full-spectrum thinking.

As recent research on the neuroscience of storytelling has concluded, our brains are wired for stories. If our brains don't hear stories, they make them up.[10] The emerging tools of full-spectrum thinking need to take this inherent need for stories into account, as they qualify sources and blend them together. Stories must be told, but they must also feed into the stories of people who are learning from clarity-filtered sources.

As a leader, you will need to perform best at the edge of your own competence, not just in your own areas of expertise. Traditionally, leaders have been expected to be at their best at the center of their expertise. Ten years from now, the edges will be more important than the center. Each task will require a blend of skills and resources that stretch beyond traditional job functions.

As we move from categorical to spectrum thinking, we will need to bridge categories and think across categories. Leaders will need strength *and* humility. Leaders are a source of clarity.

Leaders will need to seed and nurture hope. This will be especially true among young people, working across generations. Those young people who started to become adults in 2010 or later (what I refer to as the 2010 threshold) are the first true digital natives—and the younger they are, the stronger the effect. I am very optimistic about these young people, *if* they have hope. If they have hope, they will be inspiring. If they don't have hope, they will be depressed, or dangerous.

Faith can incite a feeling of power. In a distributed-authority world, the power of faith will be increasingly distributed. Individuals will feel it, organizations can grow because of it, and societies can be influenced by it. In a world where anything that can be distributed will be distributed, many will long for certainty, and there will always be somebody—usually a religious or political leader—who will promise false certainty. Expect power shifts, power struggles, and power plays focused around making meaning and using the promise of meaning as a motivator.

We are all in a dangerous game of hope.

Full-Spectrum Thinking for an Urgent Future

What Can You Do Now?

FULL-SPECTRUM THINKING IS A ROBUST WAY TO VISUAL-ize, understand, and make the future better. The future will punish categorical thinking in the long run, even if it provides short-term illusions of success. Sloppy categorical thinking, so common today, will be embarrassing in the future.

New tools, networks, and a next generation of leaders will make it much easier to practice disciplined full-spectrum thinking. Early practitioners will get a competitive advantage; later everyone will be required to do full-spectrum thinking.

This book is mostly about why full-spectrum thinking will be necessary to thrive in the future. I hope that this foresight will provoke your insight and action—whether or not you agree with my forecast. Just to keep us oriented as we cycle from foresight to insight to action in this conclusion, recall my core definition of full-spectrum thinking:

> Full-spectrum thinking is the ability
> to seek patterns and clarity

across gradients of possibility—
outside, across, beyond, or maybe even without
any boxes or categories—while resisting false certainty.

In this conclusion, I focus on *what you can do now.* I've made the case for full-spectrum thinking in this book, so what can you do to learn more, spread the word, and develop your skills? Each of the three parts of this book invites specific opportunities for action.

The Past Cannot Continue— What Can You Do Now?

Identify signals and develop a signals database of full-spectrum thinking and full-spectrum thinkers in your organization today. Reward and elevate signals awareness in any ways that you can. Look for the unevenly distributed futures that are already here in your world of today. Certainly, there are at least a few full-spectrum thinkers around you already. Certainly, there are tools that are already there to help people see beyond narrow categories of thought. Find these early expressions, reward people for them, and build on them.

Signals are those unevenly distributed futures that William Gibson was talking about when he famously said, "The future is already here, it is just unevenly distributed."[1] Signals serve as evidence to show that a future forecast or futures scenario is plausible and at least showing some sign of life already. The discipline of looking for signals encourages people to scan today's environment and identify potential seeds for tomorrow's disruption.

A signal is a recent small or local innovation—a new product, service, behavior, initiative, policy, data point, or technology—with the potential to scale in impact and disrupt other places, people, or markets. Signals are specific events or innovations happening today that are likely to take us in a new direction. Signals help capture emerging phenomena sooner than traditional social science methods.

Large-scale trends or technology domains—like AI, automation, driver-

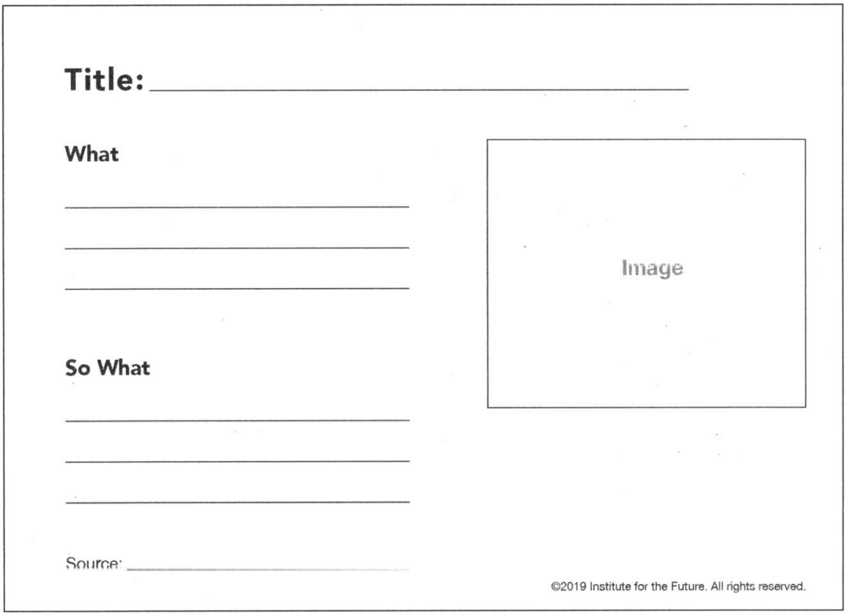

Title: _____

What

_____

_____

_____

So What

_____

_____

_____

Image

Source: _____

©2019 Institute for the Future. All rights reserved.

FIGURE 12.1: IFTF's standard template for describing signals.

less cars, or machine learning—are not signals. A big-picture future forecast is not a signal.

At IFTF we use a standard template, shown in Figure 12.1, to capture and share signals.

Start by giving your signal a title. Keep it pithy and compelling with enough bite to capture someone's attention. Next, define your "What" statement. It should be short and concise, with enough information for a total stranger to understand the general concept of your signal. The "So What" is where you link the signal to a forecast. How does the signal you've identified tell us something about the future that is starting to emerge? What new connections and patterns of understanding do you see as a result of identifying this signal? Finish by including an image or video, and remember to cite the source where you found your signal, even if it comes from a conversation with a coworker or your kids.

Here are some key rules of thumb that we use at IFTF to hone our signals tracking process:

- A good signal isn't defined by whether it becomes a commercial success or not. Many good signals fail, but the way in which they fail often reveals a future direction.

- The purpose of a signal is to help uncover an emergent motivation, behavior, or structure for the future.

- Learning to identify and develop a strong signals database takes time and practice.

- A good signal must be specific, current, compelling, and provocative.

- A good signal will have the potential to spark conversation, shift existing worldviews, spread virally, and challenge traditional authority.

Look for examples in your world of narrow categorical thinking or labeling that limits opportunity. Certainly, there are also cases where your organization and your fellow workers are judging too soon or labeling too narrowly. Expose the limits of categorical thinking in your organization, in your industry. Seek out categorical thinking and correct it wherever you can—or at least point out the limitations.

Mindset matters if you want to unlock categorical thinkers and thinking. In the early days of teleconferencing, for example, I was working with Procter & Gamble to do a trial of video teleconferencing in Cincinnati. We wanted to connect two P&G locations, one north of the city and one downtown. We went to the video teleconferencing providers of the time to find out how much it would cost to install two video teleconferencing rooms. The price was staggering. One of the P&G folks had a clever idea, however: he went to one of P&G's advertising agencies and asked them to create a television commercial set that *looked like* a video teleconferencing room so they could shoot a commercial. The cost was a fraction of what the video teleconferencing providers had offered and was just right for the trial we wanted to conduct. Mindset matters. If you're stuck in categorical thinking, you need something that breaks you out.

Encourage and reward full-spectrum thinking for all levels of learning. Full-spectrum thinking will allow people to be more future-ready, more able to make sense out of new opportunities and threats. Full-spectrum thinking will allow us to make a better future through efforts like training and executive development programs for corporations, nonprofits, government agencies, and the military.

Your goal should be to improve how people think. Encourage use of the new clarity filters to help move beyond categorical thinking. Work with local elementary schools, high schools, mentoring programs, colleges, and universities as well. Again, full-spectrum thinking is already out there, but it needs to be communicated, supported, and scaled. And don't forget, gameful engagement will be the most powerful learning medium in history. Gameful engagement is a great way to practice full-spectrum thinking.

Imbed Now, FUTURE, Next into your strategy and innovation processes. Future-back thinking makes it much easier to see full spectrum. The present is just too noisy and the lure of the past too strong. Most organizations and most leaders think Now, Next, Future—and they don't spend much time at all in Future. Full-spectrum thinkers should think Now, FUTURE, Next. Many organizations with which I work use something like Now, Next, Future as a strategy framework. Others use similar models like Horizon 1, Horizon 2, Horizon 3. Future-back thinking is a simple but profound reordering.

You should still spend most of your time on the business of now, what many companies call Horizon 1, since that's where you run your business, make money, and pursue your mission. But since it is actually easier to see where things are going if you think 10 or more years ahead, it is much better to take the Now, FUTURE, Next approach than to inch your way out from the present.

I'm often asked how I can do 10-year forecasting so accurately, since most people get stuck at 1 or 2 years ahead. The answer is because 10-year forecasting is usually easier than 1- or 2-year forecasting. The future-back view is just more clear than the present-forward view. Since future-back thinking is easier and clearer, why not do it?

The Scottish futurist and former president of Institute for the Future Ian Morrison developed what he termed the "two-curve framework" in his book *The Second Curve*.[2]

As shown in Figure 12.2, this is a simple but powerful model in which

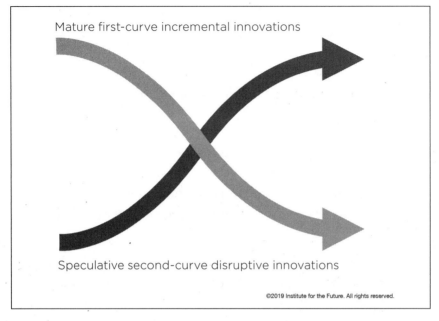

Mature first-curve incremental innovations

Speculative second-curve disruptive innovations

FIGURE 12.2: The two-curve framework.

businesses can assess their mature "first-curve" incremental (and often highly profitable) innovations versus more speculative "second-curve" disruptive innovations. The two-curve framework is a tool for navigating two kinds of strategic errors common to drawing insight from foresight. One is to jump too soon, leaving stability and still well-performing assets on the table. The other is to underestimate the pace of change and end up stuck on the first curve in decline. Scaling the second curve promotes balance.

To do a two-curve analysis, you first begin by writing an overarching From → To statement (see Figure 12.3). This statement will help you identify the change coming and what will be needed to thrive in the future.

At the top of the first curve, plot assumptions, practices, and historical strategies that support the way things are currently done. At the base of the second curve, plot today's innovations and initiatives, the internal or external signals of change. Then populate the rise of the second curve with strategies for how your organization can scale its capacity to operate in a transformational and disruptive future.

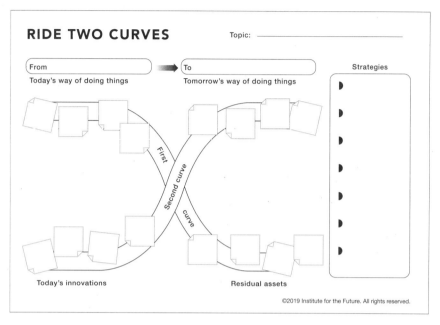

FIGURE 12.3: IFTF's template to help people apply the two-curve framework to their own situations.

At the bottom of the first curve, plot residual assets. These are current assets that may not retain their entire value but may be reusable and repurposed in new and interesting ways.

Finally, brainstorm strategies you might use to successfully transition from the first to the second curve. Figure 12.3 is a summary chart you can use to create your own two-curve analysis.[3]

New Full-Spectrum Tools, Networks, and People—What Can You Do Now?

Experiment with a range of clarity filters for a variety of purposes. Clarity filters will provide an increasingly robust lens on the information overload that all of us face. Toxic misinformation and disinformation, what has come to be called "fake news," makes the overload much worse—even if you assume good intentions, which is very hard to do for all or even most sources.

The obvious applications are information filtering for content, market, or consumer information. What information do you need to run your business? What information is most critical, and how important is it that that information is accurate?

The less obvious applications are for functions like advertising. Traditional advertising is dead already, but many companies keep trying anyway. The true digital natives will kill advertising. The kids are curators and they understand how to use clarity filters in very sophisticated ways. You cannot just push product at them, and don't call them passive "consumers." Advertisers need to learn how to engage and provide value—not just push product. A broader notion of human identity will become apparent over the next decade, and companies will need to understand and engage with people without violating their privacy.

Consider how clarity filters might be used in the next generation of advertising. Instead of just pushing products, advertisers should engage with the people who use their products and should provide value to match their products to customer needs. Clarity filters would help advertisers find the best customers, and they would help potential customers find the best providers. In this world, clarity filters will lubricate the evolution of products toward services, subscriptions, experiences, and personal or organizational transformations.

Experiment with blockchain and other forms of distributed-authority computing. Every organization should have a distributed-authority computing strategy, and blockchain is a great place to start. In a world where every transaction through a supply web can be tracked, brands will be constantly unbundled and rebundled to meet dynamic market demands.

As cryptocurrencies proliferate, new kinds of tokens will reshuffle the marketplace and perhaps societies as well—particularly where there is political turmoil. The injection of smart contracts will change the nature of business. Crowdsourced infrastructures will become much more practical with blockchains, even though blockchain is far from proven at large-scale levels. Still, blockchain is a big step in the direction of distributed-authority computing. Even its failures will be instructive over the next decade.

Smart contracts will manage more and more business activities, which will lead to new legal practices, new laws, and new types of criminality. Finally, people will develop their own smart online personas behind veils of encryption that protect the people behind the personas.[4]

My colleagues Jane McGonigal and Sam Woolley worked with Omidyar Network, the philanthropic investment firm, to design the Ethical Operating System now known as the Ethical OS. The Ethical OS is a practical framework designed to help makers of tech consider and anticipate future risks or scenarios before they happen. The Ethical OS ("or how not to regret the things you will build") is geared for product managers, engineers, and the like, and it outlines emerging risks and scenarios so that future tech designers can better future-proof their tech. When you experiment with clarity filters, blockchain, or any other new media innovations, the Ethical OS will give you a very practical framework to pursue the positives and avoid the potential negatives of your venture.

The Ethical OS embraces full-spectrum thinking about potential impacts and begins to challenge the traditional passive notion that tech designers are just designers and ought not to worry about the implications their tech could have in the wrong hands. The Ethical OS grounds its framework in the following three core questions:

1. If the technology you're building right now will someday be used in unexpected ways, how can you hope to be prepared?

2. What new categories of risk should you pay special attention to now?

3. Which design, team, or business model choices can actively safeguard users, communities, society, and your company from future risk?

The Ethical OS walks designers through three fundamental stages: imagine future risk, identify the emerging areas of social harm, and future-proof your technology to avoid potential harm. In imagining future risks, the Ethical OS draws out 14 scenarios for designers to consider, from drone delivery to predictive justice tools that automatically deliver prison sentences based on aggregate data. These scenarios help designers think through potential impacts that stem from issues inherent in our tech today: data mining, privacy, algorithmic bias, etc.

The Ethical OS identifies eight risk zones where hard-to-anticipate and unwelcome consequences are most likely to emerge:

- Truth, disinformation, and propaganda
- Addiction and the dopamine economy
- Economic and asset inequalities
- Machine ethics and algorithmic biases
- Surveillance state
- Data control and monetization
- Implicit trust and user understanding
- Hateful and criminal actors

Designers are encouraged to consider their technology innovation and identify in which risk zone their product is likely to be most vulnerable. After a risk zone is identified, designers imagine a future world and imagine their product in that world. Then designers are moved onto the final stage of the Ethical OS—attempting to future-proof their technology. For this final stage, the Ethical OS has developed six strategies that turn "best intentions into actionable safeguards." These strategies and ideas are aimed to inspire action and added infrastructure to the tech designer's environment.[5]

Recruit and promote true digital natives for leadership roles. Today's young people want to advance quickly, but often today's organizations just aren't designed to provide rapid increases in responsibility (not necessarily with titles) and reward (not necessarily with money).

The digital natives, many of whom learned full-spectrum thinking through video gaming, will have a competitive advantage over their older colleagues as they become leaders in the workforce. The rest of us will sometimes be embarrassed by our unthinking categorization of people, policies, and ideas that will be obvious to the true digital natives.

The military does a very good job of providing rapid increases in responsibility at junior levels, but many large corporations are still stuck with slow-moving career paths. Cross-generational tensions loom in this space, but there are great opportunities to flip this dilemma into an opportunity.

Develop a cross-generational mentoring program for your work force. Cross-generational mentoring is one of the most profound yet simple changes to introduce. At Institute for the Future, almost every research team is a cross-generational team. For the last 15 years, I've had a young person working very closely with me. My criterion for selecting people to work directly with me is simple: different from me in an interesting way. These young people have been mentors to me at least as much as—and often more than—I have been a mentor to them.

While the true digital natives are 24 or less in 2020, it is important to realize that everyone has something to add to the cross-generational mix. Those of us who are older have license to play the wisdom game, but we need to understand how to play that game with new media, new rules, and new dangers.

Broader Spectrums, New Applications for the Future—What Can You Do Now?

Start a new business development project on how to turn your products into services, subscriptions, experiences, and personal or organizational transformations. The idea here is simple: create a project team to study how your current products could be transformed by a service and experience mentality. Think beyond products. Think especially beyond commodity products where competition is based only on price. Consider questions like these:

- What is the value that customers experience from your product (in other words, what job is it doing for them)?
- How often do your customers experience that value?
- If only a fraction of customers' experience is perceived as valuable, how might a subscription (consider the Fender story in Chapter 7) enable a bigger fraction?

- What data does your product collect today, and what could it collect in the future that would provide value for your customers?

- What experiences are your customers seeking beyond what your current products provide?

- Are there issues of trust in your current business model, and how might trust be built into a broader subscription or service?

In Part Three of our book called *The Reciprocity Advantage*, Karl Ronn and I laid out a basic model and a checklist for exploring innovation and growth through a wide range of service and experiences businesses.

The core of the model is to first understand your right of way and your underutilized assets. Second, who might you partner with to create a new business that you could not create alone. Third, how might you create a large number of small-scale experiments to explore the possibilities? This approach is challenging for many large corporations, who are often inclined to do a small number of large experiments. Finally, only scale when the new business has a sustainable model for profitability over time. In our book, Karl Ronn created a series of checklists based on those he had first developed in his work as a disruptive innovation leader at Procter & Gamble.[6]

How might you move toward value pricing, without getting stuck in price-only competition? How might you move toward selling outcomes or ongoing experiences, rather than products? How might you move from pursuing hit products toward developing deep customer relationships over time?

Any new business development strategy will benefit from a well-thought-out roadmap that outlines where you currently stand and where you want to go. An action roadmap will address challenges and stumbling blocks that you will encounter, and force you to consider your future in terms of short-, mid-, and long-term actions. Building an action roadmap for the future will help you create a shared visual plan of action for making the future a reality. A visual action roadmap will clearly define the narrative and plan of attack for creating your future. We have found it useful to create an action roadmap using future-back strategy to understand how best to get to your desired future.

When using the template in Figure 12.4, start by populating the column

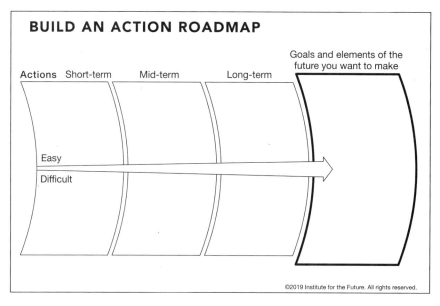

FIGURE 12.4: IFTF's template for creating action roadmaps.

on the far right with goals and elements of a future you want to build. These can be strategies, initiatives, or complete reorgs that need to happen by a certain date to make you future-ready.

Next, brainstorm actions that will help you, your team, or your company lead to your future. We recommend you use sticky notes for this process. Once you've written down a handful of actions, you will want to review and group them. Your roadmap will serve as a continuum where you can begin to plot these actions into short-, mid-, or long-term zones. If the actions you plot are easy, place them above the midline. If they are tough, place them below the midline.

After your actions have been plotted, refine actions by noting necessary decision points, needed innovations or breakthroughs, necessary investments, or new resources required in order to effectively complete your desired action.

Make sure to capture milestones or other success metrics when mid- and long-term actions are not obvious or are likely to require refining over time. Here are some rules of thumb that we use:

- Although 10 years is typical for IFTF's futures projects, it may not be right for you. In some cases, your short-, mid-, and long-term goals could be "before our next weekly meeting," "by the next all-hands meeting," and "by this time next year."

- Every stage of the roadmap should have a framing story. It may be useful to write a short narrative to bring your roadmap to life.

- Revisit your roadmap over time to remind yourself of your strategic goals, and populate each goal with more short-term action items.[7]

Create and experiment with an animated organization chart. Virtual, mixed, and augmented reality tools are making it much easier to animate an organization chart. With new blended-reality tools, people will be able to go inside an organization chart as an avatar and move around. Who is linked to whom? How are formal and informal organizational boundaries shifting? How should hierarchies come and go in response to changing business priorities? Organization charts should not be static snapshots; they should be animated movies of connectivity.

Michael Arena's book called *Adaptive Space: How GM and Other Companies Are Positively Disrupting Themselves and Transforming into Agile Organizations* is a very practical handbook for large organizations trying to become more animated. His term *adaptive space* describes how GM is reimagining itself as a successful mobility services company.

Arena introduces a "4D model" that I find both comprehensive and useful: discovery connections, development interactions, diffusion connections, and disruptive connections. These "4Ds" are organized around brokers, connectors, energizers, and challengers—all functioning in the adaptive space.[8] An animated organization chart can incorporate all four of these dimensions.

Hold a "future of HR" summit to explore human-computing resources. Consider renaming your HR function "human-computing resources (HCR)." If you create a compelling vision of the future with clarity, it will draw you toward that future. Create a range of alternative scenarios for how this new or transformed function should exist—beyond the current HR stereotypes. The human resources function has been devalued and operationalized in many organizations. Sometimes the best people avoid human resources, which I find sad when I step back and consider the name of the function: "human…resources." What could be more important than *human resources*? In the future, human resources will—inevitably—be augmented by computing resources. All human resources people will need to be digitally savvy, since digital resources will become so deeply a part of all human life.

As we look 10 years ahead, every human will be augmented in some way, and many of those ways will be dramatic. The challenge will be to find the right blending of human and computing. Again, ask What will humans do best? What will computers do best? Who will decide? There is a very important role here for a reimagined human resources function.

Human resources will yield to human-computing resources, whether we call them that or not. Right now, computing resources are separated from human resources. It is just obvious looking to the future, however, that human-computing resources must be mixed, stirred, and amplified. Full-spectrum thinking will blend humans and computers.

This is a ripe topic for an organizational summit of top leaders—and don't forget to invite the true digital natives. Better yet, ask them to organize the exchange.

Create and conduct spectrum diversity training for all staff. As I discussed in Chapter 10, diversity correlates with innovation. The diversity issues of social equity are not resolved, but the prospect for innovation introduces another kind of conversation. I believe that people and organizations should continue pressure for social equity across all kinds of diversity.

We can now make a separate yet complementary argument that spectrum diversity will increase innovation, performance, and growth. Growth may be a more powerful motivator than guilt.

Hold a "meaning in work" summit. For many people, work is already an important source of meaning. This may be particularly true for the digital natives, who work very hard if they know why they are being asked to work so hard and what they are pursuing. Meaning-making is a giant motivator for all ages in all cultures—but especially for young people, I believe.

There will be an obvious need here for work-life navigation. The higher ground is flexibility and choice, but meaning must be linked in explicit ways back to purpose.

This is another ripe topic for an organizational summit of top leaders—and don't forget the true digital natives.

Final Thoughts

Sometimes, certainty trumps truth. Saying things with certitude, however, will often trigger even greater uncertainty in the long run. In the future, people will need to trade in the certainty and the comfort of binary categories for full-spectrum thinking.

Full-spectrum thinking will provide powerful ways to make sense out of new opportunities without assuming that new experiences mirror old categories, boxes, labels, or buckets. Full-spectrum thinking will help people avoid thoughtless labeling of others. Full-spectrum thinking will be a technology-enabled antidote to polarization and simplistic thinking.

The future will be loaded with dilemmas—problems that won't go away and that you can't solve, but you have to figure out how to make things better anyway. Even in a dilemma-ridden future, we will still have to make decisions.

Full-spectrum thinking will be challenging for everyone, and we will all need low-risk ways to practice. Gameful engagement is the best way to practice, and the kids are more ready for this than the rest of us. If you categorize too soon or incorrectly, you will be in trouble. If you take too much time and cannot see a broader spectrum, you may make decisions too late. Full-spectrum thinking can animate the creative zone between premature decisions and deciding too late.

I want to seed and nurture a swelling wave of full-spectrum thinking and thinkers. My purpose is to encourage businesses, public officials, and individual people to think beyond simplistic stereotypes, labels, categories, boxes, slots, or buckets. Full-spectrum thinking will be much more nuanced than categorical thinking. And, enabled by the new mix of tools, the value of broader spectrums of thought will be scalable globally.

The scrambled future will be an asymmetrical patchwork of urgency, panic, imbalance, and hope. As the present gets more complicated, the value of full-spectrum thinking will become clearer and more urgent. Categorize when you must, but categorize with caution. Practice and grow your discipline and skills for full-spectrum thinking.

When I was presenting these ideas to a group of health care CEOs who are part of the Center for Corporate Innovation (CCI), Jeremy Boal, MD, from Mount Sinai made an insightful comment about full-spectrum thinking. He said, "Oh, you mean we will be required to see the world as it is." Amen.

This book is an optimistic forecast in a time when pessimism abounds. Full-spectrum thinking will reveal how we are connected, as well as how we are different. The challenge is for us—individuals, organizations, and society—to find our common ground in the future and pursue that positive future with clarity.

Many people have certainty, but few have clarity. You can change that.

NOTES

Introduction

1. I debate in my own mind whether to use *spectrum* or *spectra*, since I don't want to imply just one continuum. This book focuses on the value of considering a full spectrum of whatever issue, topic, idea, phenomenon, system, or any other future you confront. *Spectra* is a less familiar and less clear term, but it also implies a different way of thinking—which is exactly what I'm suggesting. *Broad spectrums* may work better for some people than *full spectrum*.

2. This notion is from John Fowles and Frank Horvat's *The Tree* (Toronto: Collins, 1979), a beautiful book that does not have page numbers.

Chapter 1

1. Peter Drucker has been referred to as the founder of modern management. He coined the term *knowledge worker* and was an early advocate of the need for lifelong learning. His long career spanned journalism, business, and academics. He wrote 39 books, including two novels and one autobiography.

Chapter 2

Psychiatrist Scott Shannon from the Wholeness Center in Fort Collins, Colorado, provided very useful reactions and suggestions on a draft of this chapter.

1. *BlacKkKlansman.* Directed by Spike Lee, Focus Features, 2018. Film.

2. Thomas S. Kuhn, *The Structure of Scientific Revolutions* (Chicago: The University of Chicago Press, 1962, 1970), page 111.

3. "Exploring the Forest Primeval and the Green Man in Our Psyche," *The Washington Post,* March 22, 2019 Issue. Web. The last portion of this quote is taken directly from John Fowles and Frank Horvat, *The Tree,* ibid. This quote is from the page with a photograph of maples, oaks, and conifers taken in October in New York State, USA.

4. From *The Tree,* Mimosas in January, Côte d'Azur, France.

5. James Prosek is an artist and writer living in Easton, Connecticut. He is the author of many books, including *Trout: An Illustrated History* and *Eels: An Exploration, from New Zealand to the Sargasso, of the World's Most Mysterious Fish.* His 2012 book, *Ocean Fishes,* is a collection of paintings of 35 Atlantic fishes, all of which were painted in life size based on individual specimens he traveled to see. Prosek has written for *The New York Times* and *National Geographic* magazine and won a Peabody Award in 2003 for his documentary about traveling through England in the footsteps of Izaak Walton, the seventeenth-century author of *The Compleat Angler.* His paintings have been shown in galleries across the country, and he is cofounder, with Yvon Chouinard, of the conservation initiative World Trout.

6. From James Prosek, *Orion Magazine,* "The Failure of Names," April 2008.

7. From personal e-mail correspondence with James Prosek: March 19, 2019.

8. Charles King, *Gods of the Upper Air: How a Circle of Renegade Anthropologists Reinvented Race, Sex, and Gender in the Twentieth Century* (New York: Doubleday, 2019), pages 4–5.

9. The *DSM-5* redefined the autism spectrum disorders to encompass the previous diagnoses of autism, Asperger syndrome, pervasive developmental disorder not otherwise specified (PDD-NOS), and childhood disintegrative disorder. https://www.aane.org/asperger-fact-sheet/

10. https://www.cio.com/article/3013221/careers-staffing/how-sap-is-hiring-autistic-adults-for-tech-jobs.html

11. UCLA Program for the Education and Enrichment of Relational Skills (PEERS) Clinic, www.semel.ucla.edu

12. https://www.xavier.edu/disability-services/x-path-program/

13. "According to Cleveland.com, future freshman Kalin Bennett is the first player with autism to receive a Division I basketball scholarship." From "NCAA's First Player with Autism Joins Kent State," by Sarah Jasmine Montgomery in Writing, But Mostly Reading@withalittlejazz. https://www.complex.com/sports/2018/11/ncaa-first-player-with-autism-joins-kent-state

14. IBID, page 27.

15. IBID.

16. ADHD is "Attention-Deficit/Hyperactivity Disorder."

17. Scott M. Shannon, MD, *Please Don't Label My Child,* New York: Rodale, 2007.

18. Amy Chua, *Political Tribes: Group Instinct and the Fate of Nations,* New York: Penguin Press, 2018, page 8–9.

19. David Frum's review of this book in the *New York Times* Book Review, March 4, 2018.

20. "The Hidden Tribes of America" is the report of a survey by The More in Common group, October 2018. https://hiddentribes.us/

21. In this case, the Berenstain Bears are building on the classic dictum in neuroscience from Donald Hebb that translates roughly as The more the neurons fire together, the more they wire together—and thus the more difficult it is to change a behavior and the more rigid we become. D. O. Hebb, *The Organization of Behavior* (New York: Wiley & Sons, 1949).

22. From Stan & Jan Berenstain, *The Berenstain Bears and the Bad Habit* (A First Time Book) (New York: Random House, 1986). I am so happy, after reading so many Berenstain Bears books to so many kids over so many years, that I can finally cite them in one of my own books.

Chapter 3

1. *VUCA* was coined at the Army War College in Carlisle, PA, where I now do guest lectures.

2. Peter Schwartz, *The Art of the Long View: Planning for the Future in an Uncertain World* (New York: Crown Business, April 15, 1996).

3. Søren Kierkegaard, *Søren Kierkegaards Skrifter: Journalen JJ:167* (Copenhagen, 1843).

4. Bob Johansen, *Get There Early: Sensing the Future to Compete in the Present* (San Francisco: Berrett-Koehler, 2007).

5. In the Conclusion, I've included a brief tutorial about how to identify and collect signals, as well as a link that shows how to learn these skills more deeply.

6. Eric Alterman, "The Decline of Historical Thinking," *The New Yorker,* February 4, 2019.

7. "The Three Horizons of Growth," *McKinsey Quarterly,* December 2009.

8. Bob Johansen, *The New Leadership Literacies: Thriving in a Future of Extreme Disruption and Distributed Everything* (Oakland: Berrett-Koehler, 2017).

9. Mark Johnson and Josh Suskewicz, *Lead from the Future: How to Turn Visionary Thinking into Breakthrough Growth* (Cambridge, MA: Harvard Business School Press, 2020).

10. Mark Weick, Lead Director, Sustainability and Enterprise Risk Management, The Dow Chemical Company, Midland, MI, quoted from e-mail correspondence to Bob Johansen, April 2, 2019.

11. Steven Johnson, *Farsighted: How We Make the Decisions That Matter the Most* (New York: Riverhead Books, 2018), page 25.

12. Willie Pietersen, *Strategic Learning: How to Be Smarter Than Your Competition and Turn Key Insights into Competitive Advantage* (Hoboken, NJ: Wiley, 2010).

13. Thomas L. Friedman, "The Answers to Our Problems Aren't as Simple as Left or Right," *The New York Times*, July 7, 2019.

14. Thomas Piketty, *Capital in the Twenty-first Century* (Cambridge, MA: Harvard University Press, 2014).

15. Sean McFate, *The New Rules of War: Victory in the Age of Durable Disorder* (New York: William Morrow, 2019), pages 8–9.

16. Thomas W. Malone, *Superminds: The Surprising Power of People and Computers Thinking Together* (New York: Little, Brown and Company, 2018).

17. Kathleen Belew, *Bring the War Home: The White Power Movement and Paramilitary America* (Cambridge, MA: Harvard University Press, 2018), page 16.

18. Tweet by William Gibson from account @GreatDismal, August 17, 2018.

19. Interview with Amanda Little conducted by Sean Illing, "The Climate Crisis and the End of the Golden Era of Food Choice," in The Highlight by Vox, June 24, 2019.

Chapter 4

1. A recent book has come out that summarizes these influences. See Patrick Parr, *The Seminarian: Martin Luther King Jr. Comes of Age* (Chicago: Lawrence Hill Books, 2018).

2. Tavis Smiley, with David Ritz, *Death of a King: The Real Story of Dr. Martin Luther King Jr.'s Final Year* (New York: Little, Brown, and Company, 2014).

3. Ira Flatow at Science Friday Initiative, WNYC Studios, https://www.science friday.com/about/. "All of our work is independently produced by the Science Friday Initiative, a non-profit organization dedicated to increasing the public's access to science and scientific information. WNYC Studios distributes our radio show, which you can catch on public radio stations across the U.S."

4. For most of my career, I have been a social scientist working with people who have much deeper technological training than I do. For this chapter, I have learned in particular from my colleagues Jeremy Kirshbaum, Alex Voto, Jamais Cascio, and Toshi Hoo. I have also found several recent books particularly helpful as I try to discern the patterns of change for the future: *AI Superpowers: China, Silicon Valley, and the New World Order* by Kai-Fu Lee; *Superminds: The Surprising Power of People and Computers Thinking Together* by Thomas W. Malone; and *Machine, Platform, Crowd: Harnessing Our Digital Future* by Andrew McAfee and Erik Brynjolfsson.

5. Kai-Fu Lee, *AI Superpowers: China, Silicon Valley, and the New World Order* (Boston: Houghton Mifflin Harcourt, 2018), page x.

6. Robert Johansen, *Groupware: Computer Support for Business Teams* (New York: The Free Press, 1988).

7. Clarity is one of the 10 future leadership skills I wrote about in *Leaders Make the Future* (San Francisco, CA: Berrett-Koehler, 2009). Clarity is also an important component of the new leadership literacy I call "looking back from the future, but acting now" in *The New Leadership Literacies*.

8. Bob Johansen, *Leaders Make the Future*, pages 56–74.

9. Robert Burton, *On Being Certain: Believing You Are Right, Even If You're Not* (New York: St. Martin's, 2008).

10. From a CNN story by Nic Robertson, February 18, 2019, from the 2019 Munich Security Conference (MSC 2019) for European leaders, diplomats, security professionals, and business leaders, called NATO at 70: An Alliance in Crisis, at Munich's Bayerischer Hof Hotel, February 18, 2019.

11. Zach Anderson, senior vice president of Global Analytics and Insights at Electronic Arts.

12. https://www.vox.com/latest-news/2019/3/22/18275913/statistical-signi ficance-p-values-explained?fbclid=IwAR3JNtqa8e9jhO2m9U49wVrbFnXh07222 O5zhtsuQPbr8iP0MNyk4fHvqHw

13. Institute for the Future. (n.d.). Introduction to Futures Thinking. Retrieved from https://www.coursera.org/instructor/janemcg

Chapter 5

1. The Advanced Research Projects Agencies, now called DARPA for Defense Advanced Research Projects Agency of the Department of Defense.

2. National Science Foundation.

3. https://www.rand.org/pubs/research_memoranda/RM3420.html

4. Madeleine Albright, *Fascism: A Warning* (New York: Harper, 2018).

5. Robert O. Work quoted in a CNN story from the NATO Munich Security Conference 2019, by Nic Robertson, February 18, 2019.

6. From "Fogged In," Michelle Dean, *New York Times Magazine*, February 4, 2018. Michelle Dean is the author of *Sharp: The Women Who Made an Art of Having an Opinion* (New York: Grove Press), published *on* April 2018.

7. Blockchain Futures: Map of the Decade 2017–2027, Institute for the Future Blockchain Futures Lab, SR-1911, 2017.

8. Vitalik Buterin, founder of the Ethereum blockchain.

9. Doug Merritt, president and CEO, Splunk, at a Center for Corporate Innovation meeting of Silicon Valley CEOs on August 28, 2018.

10. *AlphaGo*. Directed by Greg Kohs, Moxie Pictures, September 29, 2017. Film.

11. CSAIL is MIT's Computer Science and Artificial Intelligence Laboratory.

12. Vannevar Bush, "As We May Think," in *The Atlantic Monthly*, 1945.

13. I knew Doug Engelbart quite well, but I never met Steve Jobs—even though Institute for the Future did do projects for Apple while Jobs was the CEO. I understood that Steve Jobs and I were not likely to hit it off. I was studying the future, and he was making the future. I have great respect for him, but I realized that he was an executive that I didn't need to have on my side in order to work with Apple's advanced technology group, but I did need to have him not against me.

Chapter 6

1. *Ender's Game*. Directed by Gavin Hood, Summit Entertainment, 2013. Film.

2. Anthony R. Palumbi, "Hey Parents, Stop Worrying and Learn to Love 'Fortnite,'" *The Washington Post*, July 31, 2019.

3. https://lindastone.net/2009/11/30/beyond-simple-multi-tasking-continuous-partial-attention/

4. From the cover jacket of Dave Cullen, *Parkland* (New York: HarperCollins, 2019).

5. More detailed information about the study can be found in "Relationship of Childhood Abuse and Household Dysfunction to Many of the Leading Causes of Death in Adults," published in the *American Journal of Preventive Medicine* in 1998, Vol. 14, pages 245–258.

6. Institute for the Future, "Global Youth Skills: Work and Learn Paths for Future-Ready Learners," supported by the MiSK Foundation. IFTF research report SR-2076. http://www.iftf.org/fileadmin/user_upload/downloads/work-learn/GlobalYouthSkills_Final_Report_021419_sm.pdf

Part Three

1. *The Matrix*. Directed by Lana and Lilly Wachowski, Warner Bros, 1999. Film.

Chapter 7

1. B. Joseph Pine II and James H. Gilmore, *The Experience Economy: Work Is Theater and Every Business a Stage* (Cambridge, MA: Harvard Business School Press, 1999). The second edition is called *The Experience Economy*, updated ed. (Cambridge, MA: Harvard Business Review Press, 2011).

2. From a personal interview with John Padgett, March 13, 2019.

3. Sapna Maheshwari, "Let's Subscribe to That Sofa," *New York Times*, June 9, 2019, page 1.

4. Robert B. Tucker, "How Peloton Uses Consumer Insights to Drive Innovation," *Forbes*, February 28, 2019.

5. Bob Johansen and Karl Ronn, *The Reciprocity Advantage: A New Model for Innovation and Growth* (Oakland: Berrett-Koehler, 2015).

6. This forecast builds on the work done by Institute for the Future's Blockchain Futures Lab and the map of the decade 2017–2027 called "Blockchain Futures: Reshaping the World at the Intersection of Money, Technology, and Human Identity," Institute for the Future, Report SR-1911D, 2017.

Chapter 8

1. The phrase *flexive command* was first used in an official military publication in a paper, published in *Joint Force Quarterly* in 2017, by Andrew Hill and Heath Niemi, US Army War College.

2. As far as I can tell, the term does not yet occur in any official statements by military leaders, and it is not included in any military doctrine (the documents that define and describe the organization's ends, ways, and means of developing force and waging war). Still, I like it and hope that it spreads.

3. Quoted by Jason Koebler in "Society Is Too Complicated to Have a President, Complex Mathematics Suggest," *Vice*, November 7, 2016. https://mother board.vice.com/en_us/article/wnxbm5/society-is-too-complicated-to-have -a-president-complex-mathematics-suggest. For a more complete description on this theory, see Yaneer Bar-Yam, New England Complex Systems Institute, *Dynamics of Complex Systems (Studies in Nonlinearity)* (Boca Raton, FL: CRC Press, 1999).

4. Army Futures Command (AFC) Directorate of Intelligence (DOI), "Transforming Intelligence to Support 21st Century Army Modernization," White Paper, December 15, 2018, page 10.

5. IBID, page 3.

6. IBID, page 10.

7. This term was first used by Nelson Mandela in his autobiography entitled *Long Walk to Freedom* (New York: Back Bay Books, October 1, 1995).

8. The concept of servant leadership was first coined by Robert K. Greenleaf in his essay, "The Servant as Leader," first published in 1970.

9. TEDSalon Berlin 2014, in a talk where Jeremy Heimans introduces the topic of New Power. Reported and posted on the TED website in June, 2014.

Chapter 9

1. https://medium.com/@GarryKasparov/may-11-one-big-loss-for-a-man -one-giant-win-for-mankind-46bb42b8752f

2. Thomas W. Malone, *Superminds: The Surprising Power of People and Computers Thinking Together* (New York: Little, Brown and Company, 2018), page 3.

3. Jerry Useem, "At Work, Expertise Is Falling Out of Favor," *The Atlantic*, July 2019, page 12.

4. Orson Scott Card, from the Introduction to the book *Ender's Game* (Tor, 1994).

5. Thomas W. Malone, *Superminds*, IBID.

6. See Bob Johansen, *The New Leadership Literacies*, chapters 7–8.

7. See Amber Case, *Calm Technology: Principles and Patterns for Non-Intrusive Design* (Sebastopol, CA: O'Reilly Media, 2016).

8. Vicki Lostetter, personal correspondence, April 25, 2019.

Chapter 10

1. Hannah Gadsby, *Nanette*, Netflix special one-person show recorded at Sydney Opera House.

2. From the movie about Alan Turing's life called *The Imitation Game*, directed by Morten Tyldum, Black Bear Pictures, November 28, 2014.

3. Alexandra Kralick, "Skeletal Studies Show Sex, Like Gender, Exists Along a Spectrum," *Discover*, November 16, 2018.

4. Chip Conley, *Wisdom@Work: The Making of a Modern Elder* (New York: Penguin Random House, 2018), pages 209–210.

5. Nellie Bowles, "A New Luxury Retreat Caters to Elderly Workers in Tech (Ages 30 and Up)," *The New York Times*, March 4, 2019, Technology Section.

6. Institute for the Future, *The Future Is a Life Seen Through the Lens of Possibility*, sponsored by United Cerebral Palsy and BIG SKY Corporate Foundation including The Shapiro Family Foundation, The Brotman Foundation, WellPoint Foundation, Anthem Blue Cross Blue Shield Foundation, Ripplewood Holdings, and Alegent Health, Report SR-1040, 2007.

7. Phil Matier, "SF Board of Supervisors Sanitizes Language of Criminal Justice System," *San Francisco Chronicle*, August 11, 2019.

8. Scott Page, *The Difference* (Princeton, NJ: Princeton University Press, 2007).

9. https://www.vanguardstem.com. *On the Vanguard: Conversations with Women of Color in STEM*, or #VanguardSTEM for short, is a live monthly web series featuring a rotating panel of women of color in STEM discussing a wide variety of topics including their research interests, wisdom, advice, tips, tricks, and commentary on current events. This web series, and the online platform it spurred, is a signature program of The SeRCH Foundation, Inc., "a not-for-profit organization dedicated to using science, technology, engineering and mathematics (STEM) as a tool for social justice."

10. From e-mail exchanges with Anthony Weeks, February 6, 2019.

11. This forecast builds on the forecast done in 2007 by Institute for the Future called *The Future Is a Life Seen Through the Lens of Possibility*, IBID.

12. Bob Johansen, *The New Leadership Literacies*, chapters 9–10, pages 117–131.

Chapter 11

1. See Eric Hoffer's book *The True Believer: Thoughts on the Nature of Mass Movements* (New York: Harper & Brothers, originally published in 1951).

2. From a telephone conversation with Casper ter Kuile, November 30, 2018.

3. This hunger for deep explorations of meaning, values, and purpose could be one of the factors driving new interests in psychedelics over the last few years. Psychedelics promise to break us out of our categorical thinking and unveil the world in new and more profound ways. The best summary of this new perspective on psychedelics is Michael Pollan's popular book called *How to Change Your Mind: What the New Science of Psychedelics Teaches Us about Consciousness, Dying, Addiction, Depression, and Transcendence* (New York: Penguin Press, 2018). I love his opening quote from Emily Dickinson: "The soul should always stand ajar."

4. Robert Johansen and Rob Swigart, *Upsizing the Individual in the Downsized Organization* (Boston: Addison-Wesley, 1994).

5. Institute for the Future, "Good Company: What's the Meaning of Work?" SR-589, November, 1995, page 3.

6. My colleague David Pescovitz was the first person to introduce me to this positive correlation between virtual and in-person experiences. Virtual communication rarely replaces in-person, unless that is forced by some external requirement such as travel restrictions.

7. Robert N. Bellah, "Habit and History," in *Ethical Perspectives* 8 (2001)3, page 161.

8. Mark Bowden, "The Man Who Saw Inside Himself," *The Atlantic*, March 2018. https://www.theatlantic.com/magazine/archive/2018/03/larry-smarr-the-man-who-saw-inside-himself/550883/

9. From Bob Johansen, *The New Leadership Literacies*, chapters 9–10. Chapter 9 describes the literacy of creating and sustaining positive energy, while Chapter 10 is a forecast of the external future forces that will enhance the process of creating and sustaining positive energy as a leader.

10. See the work of Kendall Haven for more detail. He was part of a DARPA-funded research project on the neuroscience of storytelling that brought together neuroscientists and master storytellers. This was one of their conclusions.

Conclusion

1. There is more detail on signals in Chapter 3. Institute for the Future does nonprofit training programs that teach futures thinking tools like this in much more detail. See the IFTF website: www.iftf.org

2. Ian Morrison, *The Second Curve* (New York: Ballantine, 1996).

3. Institute for the Future does nonprofit training programs that teach futures thinking tools like this in much more detail. See the IFTF website: www.iftf.org

4. Updated and adapted from Institute for the Future, *Blockchain Futures Map of the Decade 2017–2027*, IBID.

5. Institute for the Future, "Ethical OS Toolkit: A Guide to Anticipating the Future Impact of Today's Technology, Or: How Not to Regret the Things You Will Build." Creative Commons Attribution-NonCommercial-ShareAlike 4.0 International (CC BY-NC-SA 4.0) license, www.ethicalos.org

6. Bob Johansen and Karl Ronn, *The Reciprocity Advantage*, IBID, part 3. Karl Ronn was known as "the Clayton Christensen of Procter & Gamble." His role was to create new business categories that didn't exist before, such as Swiffer, Mr. Clean Magic Eraser, and Febreze.

7. Institute for the Future does training programs that teach futures thinking tools like this in much more detail. See the IFTF website: www.iftf.org

8. Michael J. Arena, *Adaptive Space* (New York: McGraw-Hill, 2018).

BIBLIOGRAPHY

Abidi, Suhayl, and Manoj Joshi. *The VUCA Learner: Future-proof Your Relevance.* Los Angeles: SAGE, 2018. Print.

Alberts, David S., and Richard E. Hayes. "The Future of Command and Control: Understanding Command and Control." CCRP, 2006. Print.

Albright, Madeleine. *Fascism: A Warning.* New York: HarperCollins, 2018. Print.

Allen, Charles. "Community Voices: Nourishing Our Community." cumberlink .com, March 12, 2019 Issue. Web.

Alterman, Eric. "The Decline of Historical Thinking." *The New Yorker,* February 4, 2019. Print.

Arbinger Institute. *The Outward Mindset—Seeing Beyond Ourselves: How to Change Lives & Transform Organizations.* Oakland, CA: Berrett-Koehler, 2016. Print.

Arena, Michael J. *Adaptive Space: How GM and Other Companies Are Positively Disrupting Themselves and Transforming into Agile Organizations.* New York: McGraw Hill Education, 2018. Print.

Bailenson, Jeremy. *Experience on Demand: What Virtual Reality Is, How It Works, and What It Can Do.* New York: W. W. Norton & Company, 2018. Print.

Bar-Yam, Yaneer, New England Complex Systems Institute. *Dynamics of Complex Systems (Studies in Nonlinearity).* Boca Raton, FL: CRC Press, 1999. Print.

Bateson, Gregory. *Mind and Nature: A Necessary Unit.* New York: E. P. Dutton, 1979. Print.

Bateson, Nora. *Small Arcs of Large Circles: Framing Through Other Patterns.* Axminster, UK: Triarchy, 2018. Print.

Baudrillard, Jean. *Simulacra and Simulation.* Ann Arbor, MI: University of Michigan Press, 1994. Print.

Belew, Kathleen. *Bring the War Home: The White Power Movement and Paramilitary America.* Cambridge, MA: Harvard University Press, 2018. Print.

Bellah, Robert N. "Habit and History." *Ethical Perspectives,* Issue 8 (2001) 3. Print.

Berentain, Stan and Jan. *The Berenstain Bears and the Bad Habit.* New York: Random House, 1986. Print.

Berinato, Scott, and Admiral Thad Allen. "Interview: You Have to Lead from Everywhere." *Harvard Business Review,* November 2010. Web.

Block, Peter. *Stewardship: Choosing Service Over Self-Interest.* Oakland, CA: Berrett-Koehler, 2013. Print.

"The Bonobo in All of Us." *NOVA Newsletter,* December 31, 2006 Issue. Web.

Booz Allen Hamilton. "The World's Most Enduring Institutions." Booz Allen Hamilton, 2004, 20040072/12/04. Print.

Brooks, David. *The Second Mountain: The Quest for a Moral Life.* New York: Random House, 2019. Print.

Brooks, David. "Students Learn from People They Love: Putting Relationship Quality at the Center of Education." *The New York Times,* January 17, 2019 Issue. Web.

Bruni, Frank. "Will the Media Fail Again?" *The New York Times,* January 13, 2019. Print.

Callahan, Shawn. *Putting Stories to Work: Mastering Business Storytelling.* Melbourne, Australia: Pepperberg, 2016. Print.

Capra, Fritjof. *The Web of Life: A New Scientific Understanding of Living Systems.* New York: Anchor Books, 1997. Print.

Case, Amber. *Calm Technology: Principles and Patterns for Non-Intrusive Design.* Sebastopol, CA: O'Reilly Media, 2016. Print.

Chang, Emily. *Brotopia: Breaking Up the Boys' Club of Silicon Valley.* New York: Portfolio/Penguin, 2019. Print.

Chen, Milton. "The 5 Habits of Extreme Learners: We Must Empower Students to Take Control of Their Own Learning." *Education Week,* December 11, 2017. Web.

Christensen, Clayton M., Efosa Ojomo, and Karen Dillon. *The Prosperity Paradox:*

How Innovation Can Lift Nations Out of Poverty. New York: HarperCollins, 2019. Print.

Christensen, Clayton M., Taddy Hall, Karen Dillon, and David S. Duncan. *Competing Against Luck: The Story of Innovation and Customer Choice*. New York: HarperCollins, 2016. Print.

Cline, Ernest. *Ready Player One*. New York: Broadway Books, 2011. Print.

Conley, Chip. *Wisdom @ Work: The Making of a Modern Elder*. New York: Crown, 2018. Print.

Cullen, David. *Parkland: Birth of a Movement*. New York: HarperCollins, 2019. Print.

Daugherty, Paul R., and H. James Wilson. *Human + Machine: Reimagining Work in the Age of AI*. Boston, MA: Harvard Business Review Press, 2018. Print.

Davenport, Thomas H. *The AI Advantage: How to Put the Artificial Intelligence Revolution to Work*. Cambridge, MA: MIT Press, 2018. Print.

Delgado, José M. R. *Physical Control of the Mind: Toward a Psychocivilized Society*. New York: Harper & Row, 1969. Print.

Dempsey, General Martin E. "Mission Command." US Army White Paper: Unclassified. April 3, 2012. Print.

Diamond, Jared. *Upheaval: Turning Points for Nations in Crisis*. New York: Little, Brown and Company, 2019. Print.

Drechsler, Lieutenant Colonel Donald, and Colonel Charles D. Allen. "Why Senior Military Leaders Fail: And What We Can Learn from Their Mistakes." *Armed Forces Journal*, July/August 2009. Web.

Dweck, Carol S. *Mindset—The New Psychology of Success: How We Can Learn to Fulfill Our Potential*. New York: Ballantine Books, 2008. Print.

Edmondson, Amy C. *The Fearless Organization: Creating Psychological Safety in the Workplace for Learning, Innovation, and Growth*. Hoboken, NJ: John Wiley & Sons, 2019. Print

Egner, Jeremy. "'Blade Runner 2049': Harrison Ford, Ryan Gosling and the Creators Discuss the Sequel." *The New York Times*, September 8, 2017 Issue. Web.

"Eliasson Global Leadership Prize: What Do Magical Thinking, Salamander Tails, Free Will, the Human Genome, and the Universal Declaration of Human Rights Have in Common?" Tallberg Foundation. January 31, 2019. Web.

Epstein, David. *Range: Why Generalists Triumph in a Specialized World*. New York: Riverhead Books, 2019. Print.

Epstein, David. "You Don't Want a Child Prodigy." *The New York Times*, May 26, 2019. Print.

Evans, Dylan, and Oscar Zarate. *Introducing Evolutionary Psychology: A Graphic Guide.* London, UK: Clays, 2010. Print.

"Exploring the Forest Primeval and the Green Man in Our Psyche." *The Washington Post*, March 22, 2019 Issue. Web.

Eyal, Nir, with Ryan Hoover. *Hooked: How to Build Habit-Forming Products.* London, UK: Portfolio Penguin, 2014. Print.

Fowles, John, and Frank Horvat. *The Tree.* Toronto: Collins, 1979. Print.

Friedman, Thomas L. "The Answers to Our Problems Aren't as Simple as Left or Right." *The New York Times*, July 7, 2019. Print.

Frost, Michael. *Exiles: Living Missionally in a Post-Christian Culture.* Grand Rapids, MI: Baker Books, 2006. Print.

Game Developers Conference—Pocket Guide: March 18–22, 2019. San Francisco, CA: gdconf.com. Print.

Gates, Melinda. *The Moment of Lift: How Empowering Women Changes the World.* New York: Flatiron Books, 2019. Print.

Girrier, Rear Admiral Robert P., US Navy. "Thinking Across the Boxes: Warfare Will Increasingly Involve Orchestrating Cooperative Efforts." *Proceedings Magazine*, January 2010, Vol. 136/1/1,283. Web.

Govindarajan, Vijay. *The Three Box Solution: A Strategy for Leading Innovation—Create the Future, Forget the Past, and Manage the Present.* Boston, MA: Harvard Business Review Press, 2016. Print.

Gray, Mary L., and Siddharth Suri. *Ghost Work: How to Stop Silicon Valley from Building a New Global Underclass.* New York: Houghton Mifflin Harcourt, 2019. Print.

Greenleaf, Robert K. "The Servant as Leader," revised edition. South Orange, NJ: Greenleaf Center for Servant Leadership, September 30, 2015. Print.

Grenville, Bruce. *The Uncanny: Experiments in Cyborg Culture.* Vancouver, British Columbia: Vancouver Art Gallery, 2002. Print.

Groysberg, Boris, Andrew Hill, and Toby Johnson. "Which of These People Is Your Future CEO?: The Different Ways Military Experience Prepares Managers for Leadership." *Harvard Business Review*, November 2010. Web.

Guinness, Os. *Renaissance: The Power of the Gospel However Dark the Times.* Downers Grove, IL: InterVarsity, 2014. Print.

Har, Janie. "California Man Learns He's Dying from Doctor on Robot Video." WJLA, March 8, 2019. Web.

Harari, Yuval Noah. *21 Lessons for the 21st Century.* New York: Spiegel & Grau, 2018. Print.

Harris, Michael. *The End of Absence: Reclaiming What We've Lost in a World of Constant Connection.* New York: Current, 2014. Print.

Hartley, Scott. *The Fuzzy and the Techie: Why the Liberal Arts Will Rule the Digital World*. Boston, MA: Houghton Mifflin Harcourt, 2017. Print.

Haven, Kendall. *Story Smart: Using the Science of Story to Persuade, Influence, Inspire, and Teach*. Santa Barbara, CA: Libraries United, 2014. Print.

Heilweil, Rebecca. "Deus Ex Machina: Religions Use Robots to Connect with the Public—The 15th Century Had the Printing Press. Today, a Handful of Religious Institutions Are Developing Interactive Machines to Share Doctrine and Converse with the Faithful." *The Wall Street Journal*, March 28, 2019 Issue. Web.

Heimans, Jeremy, and Henry Timms. *New Power: How Power Works in Our Hyperconnected World—and How to Make It Work for You*. New York: Doubleday, 2018. Print.

Hill, Andrew, and Heath Niemi. "The Trouble with Mission Command: *Flexive Command* and the Future of Command and Control." *Joint Force Quarterly*, Vol. 86, 3rd Quarter 2017. Web.

Hill, Linda A. "Leading from Behind." *Harvard Business Review*, May 5, 2010. Web.

Hirsch, Alan. *The Forgotten Ways: Reactivating Apostolic Movements*. Grand Rapids, MI: Brazos Press, 2016. Print.

Hodges, Andrew. *Alan Turing: The Enigma—The Book That Inspired the Film "The Imitation Game."* Princeton, NJ: Princeton University Press, 1983. Print.

Hoffer, Eric. *The True Believer: Thoughts on the Nature of Mass Movements*. New York: Harper and Brothers, 1951. Print.

Hudak, Ronald P., Rebecca Russell, Mei Lin Fung, and Wayne Rosenkrans. "Federal Health Care Leadership Skills Required in the 21st Century." *Journal of Leadership Studies*, Vol. 9, No. 3, 2015. Print.

IFTF Blockchain Futures Lab. "Map of the Decade 2017–2027: Blockchain Futures—Reshaping the World at the Intersection of Money, Technology, and Human Identity." Institute for the Future, 2017, SR-1911. Print.

IFTF Foresight Studio. "IFTF Foresight Toolkit—Practical Tools for Foresight, Insight, and Action." Institute for the Future, 2018, SR-2012. Print.

IFTF Future 50. "ReModeling Trust—A Workbook Exploring Trust Models in Action." Institute for the Future, 2018, SR-2010B. Print.

IFTF Technology Horizons Program. "Toward a New Literacy of Cooperation in Business—Managing Dilemmas in the 21st Century." Institute for the Future, June 2004, SR-851A. Print.

Illing, Sean. "The Climate Crisis and the End of the Golden Era of Food Choice: What's for Dinner in a Hotter, Drier, More Crowded World?" *Vox*, June 24, 2019. Web.

Institute for the Future. "UBA—Universal Basic Assets: A Manifesto for a More
   Equitable Future." Institute for the Future, 2017, SR-1968. Print.
Institute for the Future and The Consortium of Endowed Episcopal Parishes.
   "2008–2018 Map of Future Forces Affecting the Episcopal Church." Institute
   for the Future, 2008, SR-1257. Print.
Institute for the Future and The Consortium of Endowed Episcopal Parishes.
   "The Book of Provocation: Faith Conversations in the Future." Institute for
   the Future, 2008, SR-1123. Print.
Institute for the Future and the MiSK Foundation. "Global Future Skills: Work
   + Learn Paths for Future-Ready Learners." Institute for the Future, 2018,
   SR-2060. Print.
Institute for the Future and United Cerebral Palsy. "The Future Is a Life Seen
   Through the Lens of Possibility." Institute for the Future, 2007, SR-1040.
   Print.
Ismail, Salim, with Michael S. Malone, and Yuri Van Geest. *Exponential Organiza-
   tions: Why New Organizations Are Ten Times Better, Faster, and Cheaper Than Yours
   (and What to Do about It)*. New York: Diversion Books, 2014. Print.
Jenkins, Philip. *The Next Christendom: The Coming of Global Christianity*. New York:
   Oxford University Press, 2011. Print.
Jesuthasan, Ravin, and John W. Boudreau. *Reinventing Jobs: A 4-Step Approach for
   Applying Automation to Work*. Boston, MA: Harvard Business Review Press, 2018.
   Print.
Johansen, Bob. *Get There Early: Sensing the Future to Compete in the Present—Using
   Foresight to Provoke Strategy and Innovation*. San Francisco, CA: Berrett-Koehler,
   2007. Print.
Johnson, Mark, and Josh Suskewicz. *Lead from the Future: How to Turn Visionary
   Thinking into Breakthrough Growth*. Cambridge, MA: Harvard Business School
   Press, 2020. Print.
Johnson, Steven. *Farsighted: How We Make the Decisions That Matter the Most*. New
   York: Riverhead Books, 2018. Print.
Johnston, Douglas. *Faith-Based Diplomacy: Trumping Realpolitik*. New York: Oxford
   University Press, 2003. Print.
Kahneman, Daniel. *Summary: Thinking, Fast and Slow*. Redwood City, CA: Epic!
   Books, 2019. Print.
Kamenetz, Anya. *The Art of Screen Time: How Your Family Can Balance Digital Media
   & Real Life*. New York: PublicAffairs, 2018. Print.

Kasparov, Garry, with Mig Greengard. *Deep Thinking: Where Machine Intelligence Ends and Human Creativity Begins.* New York: PublicAffairs, 2017. Print.

Kaur, Rupi. *Milk and Honey.* Kansas City, MO: Andrews McMeel, 2015. Print.

Kaur, Rupi. *The Sun and Her Flowers.* Kansas City, MO: Andrews McMeel, 2017. Print.

Kelly, Kevin. *The Inevitable: Understanding the 12 Technological Forces That Will Shape Our Future.* New York: Viking, 2016. Print.

Kelly, Kevin. *Out of Control: The Rise of Neo-Biological Civilization.* Reading, MA: Addison-Wesley, 1994. Print.

King, Charles. *Gods of the Upper Air: How a Circle of Renegade Anthropologists Reinvented Race, Sex, and Gender in the Twentieth Century.* New York: Doubleday, 2019. Print.

Klein, JoAnna. "Romeo the Frog Finds His Juliet. Their Courtship May Save a Species—The Lonely Male in a Bolivian Museum Was Thought to Be the Last Sehuencas Water Frog, but an Expedition Has Found Him a Potential Mate." *The New York Times,* January 17, 2019 Issue. Web.

Koebler, Jason. "Society Is Too Complicated to Have a President, Complex Mathematics Suggest." *Motherboard—Vice,* November 7, 2016. Web.

Kolbert, Elizabeth. "Why Facts Don't Change Our Minds: New Discoveries about the Human Mind Show the Limitations of Reason." *The New Yorker,* February 27, 2017 Issue. Web.

Kotre, John. *Make It Count: How to Generate a Legacy That Gives Meaning to Your Life.* New York: Free Press, 1999. Print.

Kuhn, Thomas S. *The Structure of Scientific Revolutions.* Chicago: University of Chicago Press, 1970. Print.

Lafley, A. G. "Managing Organizations: What Only the CEO Can Do." *Harvard Business Review,* May 2009. Web.

Lawson, Steve. "Monk Manual." Cincinnati, OH: monkmanaul.com, 2019. Print.

Le, Linh K. "Examining the Rise of Hatsune Mike: The First International Virtual Idol." *The UCI Undergraduate Research Journal,* 2016, pages 1–12. Web.

Leaf, Caroline. *Think, Learn, Succeed: Understanding and Using Your Mind to Thrive at School, the Workplace, and Life.* Grand Rapids, MI: Baker Books, 2018. Print.

Lee, Kai-Fu. *AI Super-Powers: China, Silicon Valley, and the New World Order.* New York: Houghton Mifflin Harcourt, 2018. Print.

Lepore, Jill. "Annals of Media—Hard News: The State of Journalism." *The New Yorker,* January 28, 2019. Print.

Lerner, Sarah (editor and MSD teacher). *Parkland Speaks: Survivors from Marjory*

Stoneman Douglas Share Their Stories. New York: Crown Books for Young Readers, 2019. Print.

Lieberman, Matthew D. *Social: Why Our Brains Are Wired to Connect.* New York: Crown, 2013. Print.

Lincoln Park Zoo. "Nature of War: Chimps Inherently Violent; Study Disproves Theory That 'Chimpanzee Wars' Are Sparked by Human Influence." *Science Daily,* September 17, 2014 Issue. Web.

Lockheed Martin. "Full Spectrum Leadership—Full Spectrum Leadership Is the Cornerstone of Leadership at Lockheed Martin." www.lockheedmartin.com/en-us/who-we-are/leadership-governance/full-spectrum-leadership.html, 2019. Web.

Lopez, Shane J. *Making Hope Happen: Create the Future You Want for Yourself and Others.* New York: Atria Paperback, 2013. Print.

Lukianoff, Greg, and Jonathan Haidt. *The Coddling of the American Mind: How Good Intentions and Bad Ideas Are Setting Up a Generation for Failure.* New York: Penguin, 2018. Print.

Lynn, Andrew. *Generativity: The Art and Science of Exceptional Achievement.* USA: Howgill House, 2017. Print.

Maheshwari, Sapna. "Let's Subscribe to That Sofa." *The New York Times,* June 9, 2019. Print.

Malone, Thomas W. *Superminds: The Surprising Power of People and Computers Thinking Together.* New York: Little, Brown and Company, 2018. Print.

Mandela, Nelson. *Long Walk to Freedom: The Autobiography of Nelson Mandela.* New York: Back Bay Books, 1995. Print.

McAdams, Dan P., and Ed de St. Aubin. *Generativity and Adult Development: How and Why We Care for the Next Generation.* Washington, DC: American Psychological Association, 1998. Print.

McAfee, Andrew, and Erik Brynjolfsson. *Machine Platform Crowd: Harnessing Our Digital Future.* New York: W. W. Norton & Company, 2017. Print.

McChrystal, General Stanley (US Army, Ret.), Jeff Eggers, and Jason Mangone. *Leaders: Myth and Reality.* New York: Portfolio/Penguin, 2018. Print.

McChrystal, General Stanley (US Army, Ret.), with Tantum Collins, David Silverman, and Chris Fussell. *Team of Teams: New Rules of Engagement for a Complex World.* New York: Portfolio/Penguin, 2015. Print.

McFate, Sean. *The New Rules of War: Victory in the Age of Durable Disorder.* New York: HarperCollins, 2019. Print.

McMaster, Lieutenant General H. R. "Continuity and Change: The Army

Operating Concept and Clear Thinking about Future War." *Military Review*, March–April 2015, Vol. 95, No. 2. Web.

McRaven, Admiral William H. (US Navy, Ret.). *Sea Stories: My Life in Special Operations*. New York: Grand Central, 2019. Print.

Meade, Michael. *The World Behind the World: Living at the Ends of Time*. Seattle, WA: GreenFire, 2008. Print.

Menzel, Peter, and Faith D'Aluisio. *Robo sapiens: Evolution of a New Species*. Cambridge, MA: MIT Press, 2001. Print.

Miodownik, Mark. *Liquid Rules: The Delightful & Dangerous Substances That Flow Through Our Lives*. Boston, MA: Houghton Mifflin Harcourt, 2019. Print.

Morris, Craig L. *Right Side Up: Is a Better Life Possible?* Bloomington, IN: WestBow, 2016. Print.

Neumeier, Marty. *Scramble: How Agile Strategy Can Build Epic Brands in Record Time*. Parker, CO: Level C Media, 2018. Print.

Palfrey, John, and Urs Gasser. *Born Digital: Understanding the First Generation of Digital Natives*. Philadelphia, PA: Basic Books, 2008. Print.

Parr, Patrick. *The Seminarian: Martin Luther King Jr. Comes of Age*. Chicago, IL: Lawrence Hill Books, 2018. Print.

Peiser, Jaclyn. "As A.I. Reporters Arrive, the Other Kind Hangs In." *The New York Times*, February 5, 2019. Print.

Petzold, Charles. *The Annotated Turing: A Guided Tour through Alan Turing's Historic Paper on Computability and the Turing Machine*. Indianapolis, IN: Wiley, 2008. Print.

Pine, B. Joseph, II, and James H. Gilmore. *The Experience Economy:* updated ed. Boston, MA: Harvard Business Review Press, 2011. Print.

Pine, B. Joseph, II, and James H. Gilmore. *The Experience Economy: Work Is Theatre and Every Business a Stage*, 1st edition. Boston, MA: Harvard Business School Press, 1999. Print.

Pink, Sophia. "America at 21—6,000 Miles, 24 States, 8 Questions." Stanford University Speakers Bureau. November 16, 2018. Live Discussion.

Pollan, Michael. *How to Change Your Mind: What the New Science of Psychedelics Teaches Us about Consciousness, Dying, Addiction, Depression, and Transcendence*. New York: Penguin, 2018. Print.

Poynton, Robert. *Do/Improvise/Less Push. More Pause. Better Results. A New Approach to Work (and Life)*. London, UK: Do Book Company, 2013. Print.

Prosek, James. *Eels: An Exploration, from New Zealand to the Sargasso, of the World's Most Mysterious Fish*. New York: Harper Perennial, 2010. Print.

Prosek, James. "The Failure of Names." *Orion Magazine*, April 2008 Issue. Web.

Rock, David. *Your Brain at Work: Strategies for Overcoming Distraction, Regaining Focus, and Working Smarter All Day Long.* New York: HarperCollins, 2009. Print.

Rosling, Hans, with Ola Rosling and Anna Rosling Rönnlund. *Factfulness: Ten Reasons We're Wrong about the World—And Why Things Are Better Than You Think.* New York: Flatiron Books, 2018. Print.

Rothman, Joshua. "Department of First Principles: Choose Wisely—Do We Make the Big Decisions—Or Do They Make Us?" *The New Yorker,* January 21, 2019. Print.

Rubrich, Larry. "A3 Problem Solving: What It Is…And What It Isn't." *Reliable Plant,* February 9, 2019 Issue. Web.

Sagal, Peter. *The Incomplete Book of Running.* New York: Simon & Schuster, 2018. Print.

Saldanha, Tony. *Why Digital Transformations Fail: The Surprising Disciplines of How to Take Off and Stay Ahead.* Oakland, CA: Berrett-Koehler, 2019. Print.

Sardar, Ziauddin. "Welcome to Postnormal Times." *Futures,* https://doi.org/10.1016/j.futures.2009.11.028

Sardar, Ziauddin, and John A. Sweeney. "The Three Tomorrows of Postnormal Times." *Futures,* http://dx.doi.org/10.1016/j.futures.2015.10.004

Saslow, Eli. *Rising Out of Hatred: The Awakening of a Former White Nationalist.* New York: Doubleday, 2018. Print.

Schar, Mark. "Classroom Belonging and Student Performance in the Introductory Engineering Classroom." American Society for Engineering Education, Paper ID #18164, 2017. Web.

Schein, Edgar H., and Peter A. Schein. *Humble Leadership: The Power of Relationships, Openness, and Trust.* Oakland, CA: Berrett-Koehler, 2018. Print.

Shannon, Joel. "Doctor Delivers End-of-Life News Via 'Robot,' Leaving Family Frustrated." *USA Today,* March 9, 2019 Issue. Web.

Shannon, Scott M. *Mental Health for the Whole Child: Moving Young Clients from Disease & Disorder to Balance & Wellness.* New York: W. W. Norton & Company, 2013. Print.

Shannon, Scott M., with Emily Heckman. *Parenting the Whole Child: A Holistic Child Psychiatrist Offers Practical Wisdom on Behavior, Brain Health, Nutrition, Exercise, Family Life, Peer Relationships, School Life, Trauma, Medication, and More.* New York: W. W. Norton & Company, 2013. Print.

Shannon, Scott M., with Emily Heckman. *Please Don't Label My Child: Break the Doctor-Diagnosis-Drug Cycle and Discover Safe, Effective Choices for Your Child's Emotional Health.* New York: Rodale, 2007. Print.

Slusser, Susan. "The John Madden of Gaming 'Casters'—Graham, a.k.a. 'DJ Wheat,' Fills Niche as Video Game Commentator." *San Francisco Chronicle*, Section B, January 13, 2018. Print.

Smiley, Tavis, with David Ritz. *Death of a King: The Real Story of Dr. Martin Luther King Jr.'s Final Year.* New York: Little, Brown and Company, 2014. Print.

Smith, Benjamin, Nathan Senge, and Chuck Peters. *The Way of Generativity: From Separation to Resonance.* Amazon (CreateSpace), 2017. Print.

Smith, Khalil. "The NLI Business Case: How Diversity Defeats Groupthink— Smarter Thinking Isn't about You. It's about Your Team." NeuroLeadership Institute, 2019. Print.

Szpunar, Karl K., R. Nathan Spreng, and Daniel L. Schacter. "A Taxonomy of Prospection: Introducing an Organizational Framework for Future-Oriented Cognition." *PNAS*, Vol. 111, No. 52, December 30, 2014. Web.

Tatum, Beverly Daniel. *"Why Are All the Black Kids Sitting Together in the Cafeteria?"—And Other Conversations about Race.* New York: Basic Books, 1997. Print.

ter Kuile, Casper. "Content Is Everywhere. We Need Containers." On Being Impact Lab, January 11, 2019. Web.

———. "Grief as a Strategy for Social Change." On Being Impact Lab, January 25, 2019. Web.

———. "Medieval Sworn Brothers: A Model for Committed Friendship?" On Being Impact Lab, January 18, 2019. Web.

ter Kuile, Casper, and Angie Thurston. "How We Gather." https://sacred.design, 2019, pages 3–24. Web.

———. "Something More." www.howwegather.org, 2019, pages 3–24. Web.

ter Kuile, Casper, Angie Thurston, and Rev. Sue Phillips. "Care of Souls." www .howwegather.org, 2019, pages 3–23. Web.

Tillich, Paul. *The Shaking of the Foundations: In a Language Avoiding Traditional Terms a Great Theologian Addresses Himself to the Personal and Social Problems of Today.* New York: Charles Scribner's Sons, 1948. Print.

Treuer, David. *The Heartbeat of Wounded Knee: Native America from 1890 to the Present.* New York: Riverhead Books, 2019. Print.

Twenge, Jean M. "Have Smartphones Destroyed a Generation? More Comfortable Online Than Out Partying, Post-Millennials are Safer, Physically, Than Adolescents Have Ever Been. But They're on the Brink of a Mental-Health Crisis." *The Atlantic*, September 2017 Issue. Web.

———. *iGen: Why Today's Super-Connected Kids Are Growing Up Less Rebellious, More Tolerant, Less Happy—and Completely Unprepared for Adulthood—and What That Means for the Rest of Us.* New York: Atria Books, 2017. Print.

Tzuo, Tien, with Gabe Weisert. *Subscribed: Why the Subscription Model Will Be Your Company's Future—and What to Do about It.* New York: Portfolio/Penguin, 2018. Print.

US Department of Health and Human Services, and the Centers for Disease Control and Prevention. "Asperger Syndrome—Fact Sheet." www.cdc.gov/actearly, 2019. Web.

———. "Autism Spectrum Disorders—Fact Sheet." www.cdc.gov/actearly, 2019. Web.

Useem, Jerry. "At Work, Expertise Is Falling Out of Favor—These Days, It Seems, Just about All Organizations Are Asking Their Employees to Do More with Less. Is That Actually a Good Idea?" *The Atlantic,* July 2019 Issue. Web.

Useem, Michael. "Four Lessons in Adaptive Leadership." *Harvard Business Review,* November 2010. Web.

Vanier, Jean. *Community and Growth.* Mahwah, NJ: Paulist Press, 1989. Print.

Vantrappen, Herman, and Frederic Wirtz. "Organizational Structure: When to Decentralize Decision Making, and When Not To." *Harvard Business Review,* December 26, 2017. Web.

Watson, Peter. *A Terrible Beauty: The People and Ideas That Shaped the Modern Mind—A History.* London, UK: Orion Books, 2001. Print.

Weil, David. *The Fissured Workplace: Why Work Became So Bad for So Many and What Can Be Done to Improve It.* Cambridge, MA: Harvard University Press, 2017. Print.

Weiss, Jeff, Aram Donigian, and Jonathan Hughes. "Extreme Negotiations: What U.S. Soldiers in Afghanistan Have Learned about the Art of Managing High-Risk, High-Stakes Situations." *Harvard Business Review,* November 2010. Web.

Wu, Tim. *The Curse of Bigness: Antitrust in the New Gilded Age.* New York: Columbia Global Reports, 2018. Print.

ACKNOWLEDGMENTS

Steve Piersanti at Berrett-Koehler is better than the best editor I could imagine. He has an egoless style of constructive criticism that is just the right balance for me of encouragement and challenge. All of the core ideas in this book have benefited from Steve's elegant thinking.

Gabe Cervantes joined me as a research assistant just as I was getting rolling on this book, and he has been a close colleague at each stage. His mind is expansive and very good at looking for ways of understanding patterns of thought that have no frame of reference yet. Gabe knows how to connect the dots. Gabe contributed at all levels of this book except the actual writing, from big ideas to small details.

Ashley Hemstreet manages my time and travel in such an effective and efficient way that I have the time to write books. I have worked with her for years and I am amazed every day by how she is able to coordinate and organize so elegantly.

Many colleagues have reviewed drafts of this book and discussed the core ideas with me, including Eric Moore, Toshi Hoo, Jamais Cascio, Jacques Vallée, Alex Voto, Jeremy Kirshbaum, and Mark Schar.

My colleagues at Institute for the Future have been so valuable to me over the years. This book has benefited directly from the ongoing forecasts at IFTF, but I am responsible for any mistakes in understanding. These staff members have been particularly helpful to my understanding of the emerging future: Jake Dunagan, Max Elder, Julie Ericsson, Rod Falcon, Susanne Forchheimer, Alyssa Andersen, Mark Frauenfelder, Ben Hamamoto, Dylan Hendricks, Georgia Gillan, Ben Gansky, Katie Joseff, Bradley Kreit, Salley Westergaard, Daria Lamb, Carol Neuschul, Ayca Guralp, Mike Liebhold, Jane McGonigal, Sean Ness, David Pescovitz, Barry Pousman, Sara Skvirsky, Sarah Smith, Ilana Lipsett, Cindy Baskin, Quinault Childs, Lindy Willis, Anmol Chaddha, Lawrence Choi, Namsah Kargbo, Maureen Kirchner, Neela Lazkani, Rachel Maguire, Vanessa Mason, Nick Monaco, Amber Case, Nic Weidinger, and Kathi Vian.

Institute for the Future's board works tirelessly to contribute to IFTF's ongoing efforts to make the future a better place. My deep thanks to you all: Steve Milovich, Michael Kleeman, Karen Edwards, Jean Hagan, Katie Fuller, Lyn Jeffery, Marianne Jackson, Marina Gorbis, Lawrence Wilkinson, David Thigpen, and Berit Ashla.

Karen Edward's work on SoapAI was particularly inspiring for me. Karen understands the need for full-spectrum thinking at a very personal level, and her design genius is to prototype new tools and networks to do clarity filtering.

Marina Gorbis, IFTF's executive director, has encouraged me at every step in this process. Thanks also to Jean Hagan, who guided the creative process for the jacket design, Robin Bogott, and Trent Kuhn for all their help with visual communication of these ideas. Archie Ferguson did the wonderful cover design, as he has for my last three books. Lisa Mumbach made very helpful suggestions on that design and execution.

The Berrett-Koehler team has been so supportive and so constructive at each step of the way. Thanks in particular to Jeevan Sivasubramaniam, Dave Peattie of BookMatters, and wonderful copyeditor Lou Doucette.

Outside reviewers of drafts were very helpful to me and I am so grateful to them, including Erik Krogh, Kristian Simsarian, Paul Steward, Scott Shannon, Masharika Prejean Maddison, Helge Jacobson, Michael Zea, and Roger Peterson.

Casper ter Kuile, Angie Thurston, and Sue Phillips of the Sacred Design Lab, which started at the Harvard Divinity School, have inspired me to think more broadly and creatively about new spectrums of meaning. You will see reference to their work in Chapter 11.

I have learned so much from my many experiences at the Army War College, both in Carlisle and in Washington, DC. Currently, I am a guest lecturer for the Senior Seminar, mentored by General (Ret.) David M. Rodriguez and strategic coach Lieutenant General (Ret.) James Campbell. Edmund L. "Cliffy" Zukowski has been my guide for these experiences. In these sessions, I get to work with the new three-star generals on their first week in Washington. I have come away so impressed with them and so grateful for their efforts to make the future a better place for us all.

AG Lafley reviewed my telling of the Peter Drucker story in Chapter 1 and made very helpful suggestions.

Ken Hodder from the Salvation Army was so helpful to me as I wrote Chapter 11 on new spectrums of meaning.

Tessa Finlev did very moving and insightful research at Institute for the Future on spectrum diversity, and I benefited greatly from her work.

Vicki Lostetter reviewed Chapter 9 for me and was extremely helpful in her advice about the future of the human resources function.

Anthony Weeks worked with me intensively on the basic framing of the book as well as Chapter 10 to help me understand the issues of diversity and inclusion. In particular, he helped me understand the pros and cons of categorizing ourselves and others.

My first job as a research assistant was to Professor Jesse H. Brown, a professor of Old Testament. I got to sit in his office at a small desk with him. I still remember the floor-to-ceiling bookshelves and the excitement of talking about the past and the future with him. I still think of Jesse in my study, with floor-to-ceiling bookshelves that remind me of him.

I am a big believer in the human energy of coffee shops, and I give profound thanks to Kaffeehaus in San Mateo and Caffe Destino in Portland. Much of this book was written under the influence of their wonderful cappuccino.

INDEX

ABOUT THE AUTHOR

As I was writing this book, I looked back on my life and recognized specific periods, events, and people who were important when my spectrum of thought broadened dramatically. These were the periods in my life that attuned me to what I now call full-spectrum thinking. In telling you "about the author," I've decided to share some of those times instead of doing a conventional biography. I hope that this recalling of my experience will help you recall your own personal broader-spectrum disruptions. Each of these times was a reckoning for me, a realization that I had to make new choices given the new spectrum that was opening for me.

I came to Silicon Valley before it was called that, and I became an adult in this idea-fertile climate. I've been based all along at Institute for the Future, the longest-running futures think tank in the world, but I've had multiple careers working from that base, and I continue to work there full-time.

I was born in a small town in rural Illinois. My youthful life was almost completely focused on basketball in a basketball-crazy part of the country. It wasn't until I left Geneva that I faced my first reckoning that challenged the comfortable but narrow categories of thought to which I had become accustomed.

I became an all-state player and was fortunate to attend the University of Illinois on a full scholarship, but I was only a marginal Big Ten player and not nearly good enough to be a pro. One Saturday night in the old Chicago Stadium in front of 20,000 people, I was playing against UCLA and Kareem Abdul-Jabbar (then Lew Alcindor). I played pretty well, but he had an effortless 45 points. I remember looking way up at him as we stood at the free throw lane and thinking, "I need another career." All my life to that point, I had focused on basketball as core to my identity, but that part of me was over.

On a hot day in September of 1967, after graduating from Illinois, I was driving alone on the eastbound Pennsylvania Turnpike in my aging white Ford with most of my belongings in the trunk. I had no idea what was next for me. I was not attracted to any career path going forward after college. I had accepted a fellowship at Crozer Theological Seminary in Chester, Pennsylvania—the same divinity school that Martin Luther King Jr. attended. It turned out that Crozer in the late 60s was a hotbed for full-spectrum thinking, although they didn't call it that back then.

I was a strange and unlikely divinity school student, since I was going on a fellowship for students with an interest in religion and spirituality—but no commitment to the ministry. I finished with the academic credentials to be ordained, but I chose not to do that. I have a continuing interest in things spiritual, but I'm not an advocate of any brand of religion.

While in divinity school, I was a research assistant for a global conference on religion and the future. I got to carry the bags and talk informally to the world's leading futurists. My world broadened dramatically during that conference. I have a vivid memory of running beneath the helicopter blades of futurist Herman Kahn's helicopter to pick up his briefcase. During the conference on religion and the future, I remember thinking about all those fascinating futurists and saying to myself, "That's what I want to do." Somehow, five years later, I was invited to join Institute for the Future, and I've been a futurist ever since. Crozer was focused on preparing ministers and professors of religion, but instead it catapulted me into the world of futures thinking.

I did my PhD at Northwestern University. I had thought when I arrived in Evanston that I would become a professor of sociology of religion. Garrett Theological Seminary was the graduate school of religion for Northwestern at the time, and there was a hedge between the towering gargoyled Garrett and the low, sleek Vogelback Computing Center, which housed one of the world's largest computers at the time. I walked through that hedge almost every day and it was magical: it opened me to the new spectrum of network computing, just as the internet was hatching. That hedge was like the corn rows in the movie *Field of Dreams* for me.

One of my first big projects at Institute for the Future was working with the NYU Alternate Media Center in the late 1970s to explore the use of new telecommunications media with people who have developmental disabilities like cerebral palsy. My categories of thought were disrupted in that project when I met a young man with cerebral palsy. He could not speak or use his arms very well, but he communicated with a small board with the alphabet and numbers printed on it. With his feet as we sat on the floor, he was able to spell out words and communicate with me. I was amazed as, very quickly, we were able to have a conversation about the new project and how he might participate. That experience opened a new spectrum of thought for me about people with disabilities and my unexamined assumptions about what is normal. The digital aids for people with disabilities are much better now, as is our awareness of the capacities of people with developmental disabilities.

A few times in my life, it has been a single person who opened me to new spectrums of thought. When I came to IFTF, I got to work for and with Jacques Vallée, the French computer scientist and astronomer who was the role model for the scientist in the movie *Close Encounters of the Third Kind*. Jacques was unlike anyone I had ever met, and he had a spectrum of thought beyond what I could imagine. Jacques drove an old Jeep because he was constantly on call when someone reported an abduction or any kind of "close encounter." One day, Jacques took our research team to a modern art exhibit in San Francisco called the *Videola* that reimagined television as consciousness-altering multimedia, not just a content carrier. The *Videola* suggested that television was just a hint of the multimedia world of the future. More importantly, Jacques was able to immerse our team in new experiences that challenged our categories of thought. Over my life, I've gotten to work with a small handful of people who disrupted my spectrums of thought in profound ways.

From 1996 to 2004 I was president of Institute for the Future in a time of crisis. I had studied leadership and led small teams, but now I was in charge of the entire Institute. Another spectrum opened around questions like these: How do we find funding to support such a long-term view of the future? What organizational structure makes the most sense, and what kind of offices should we have in which locations? What should be acceptable behavior within a futures think tank? There were no easy answers to any of these questions, yet somehow we made it through and the Institute is still going strong.

While I was leading IFTF, I went to China frequently in an effort to collaborate with futures thinking efforts there. On my first trip, I remember reading an article on the "socialist market economy." I had thought, up to that point, that socialist or market economy was a binary choice—not a spectrum of possibilities. I was wrong.

In Chapter 8, I talked about my experience at the Army War College in Carlisle, Pennsylvania, the week before 9/11. Since then, I have brought corporate and nonprofit leaders to the college for three-day immersive learning experiences focused on leadership and learning. For many of us, the experiences in Carlisle and at Gettysburg have been life changing. I grew up very skeptical about the military, but I have learned so much from them. I had categorized them incorrectly and unfairly. That experience in Carlisle changed my life.

For most of my career, I have traveled intensively. One of my coping techniques has always been to imagine all the things that could go wrong and be very aware of my surroundings. My military friends call this situation awareness. In 2010, I did a keynote talk in London on the VUCA World (Volatile, Uncertain, Complex, and Ambiguous) and cloud computing. That afternoon, air traffic was closed down over most of Europe because of a volcanic ash cloud from an eruption in Iceland. From April 15 to April 23, I was stranded in London, one day at a time with no knowledge of when flying would become possible again, while scrambling to arrange for alternative speakers for the events I was missing in other cities. This experience taught me that I could never imagine all the things about travel that could go wrong. I wish I could say that I used the time very creatively (I was working on a book), but instead I stewed, pondered what to do next, and watched the BBC for the latest news. The tools of foresight only go so far, and I'm not always good at applying them to myself.

In 2014, I had an experience that broadened my spectrum of thinking about the profit motive. I wrote a book called *The Reciprocity Advantage* with Karl Ronn, the Procter & Gamble innovator behind products like Febreze, Swiffer, Mr. Clean Magic Eraser, and many more. Karl taught me that business is not a zero-sum game where one competitor wins and the others lose. Rather, give-to-get logic can work in surprising ways to promote innovation where there are multiple winners.

Writing *Full-Spectrum Thinking* has given me a new lens on my own life, and I hope the book will do that for you as well. I also hope that it will help you be more open and engaged in the next moment when you are drawn toward full-spectrum thinking.

Think back over your own life. What were the moments of reckoning, when new spectrums of opportunity or threat opened for you?

ABOUT
INSTITUTE FOR THE FUTURE

Institute for the Future is the world's leading futures-thinking organization whose mission is to disrupt short-termism and demonstrate the value of urgent foresight to provoke actionable insight.

For over 50 years, businesses, governments, and social impact organizations have depended upon IFTF global forecasts, custom research, and foresight training to navigate complex change and develop world-ready strategies. IFTF was a spin-off of Rand Corporation and the Stanford Research Institute (now SRI International). It was formed during the very early days of the internet, a time that is discussed in detail in Chapter 5 on distributed-authority networks.

IFTF harnesses futures thinking by using years of experience, research, methodologies, and toolsets to yield coherent views of transformative possibilities across all sectors that together support a more sustainable and equitable future.

IFTF conducts custom forecasts for companies, government agencies, and nonprofits, as well as public and custom training programs to help people cultivate essential new skillsets and visionary mindsets to enable a better collective future. These are futures-thinking tools that help people think like futurists, to develop uncommonly coherent, compelling views of the future. Join IFTF today to unleash the power of futures thinking for all.

Institute for the Future is a registered 501(c)(3) nonprofit organization based in downtown Palo Alto, California.

For more information, see www.iftf.org.

Also by Bob Johansen

Leaders Make the Future, Second Edition

Ten New Leadership Skills for an Uncertain World

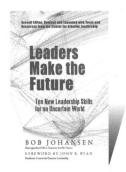

We are in a time of accelerating disruptive change. In a VUCA world—one characterized by volatility, uncertainty, complexity, and ambiguity—traditional leadership skills won't be enough, noted futurist Bob Johansen argues. Drawing on the latest forecasts from the Institute for the Future—the first futures think tank ever to outlive its forecasts—this powerful book explores the external forces that are shaking the foundations of leadership and unveils ten critical new leadership skills.

Hardcover, ISBN 978-1-60994-487-2
PDF ebook, ISBN 978-1-60994-488-9
ePub ebook, ISBN 978-1-60994-489-6

The New Leadership Literacies

Thriving in a Future of Extreme Disruption and Distributed Everything

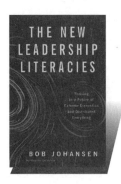

Over the next decade, today's connected world will be explosively more connected. Most leaders—and most organizations—aren't ready for this future. This visionary book provides a vivid description of the ideal talent profile for future leaders. To get ready for this onslaught of rapid change, we will all need new leadership literacies.

Hardcover, ISBN 978-1-62656-961-4
PDF ebook, ISBN 978-1-62656-962-1
ePub ebook, ISBN 978-1-62656-963-8

Berrett–Koehler Publishers, Inc.
www.bkconnection.com

800.929.2929

Berrett–Koehler
Publishers

Berrett-Koehler is an independent publisher dedicated to an ambitious mission: *Connecting people and ideas to create a world that works for all.*

Our publications span many formats, including print, digital, audio, and video. We also offer online resources, training, and gatherings. And we will continue expanding our products and services to advance our mission.

We believe that the solutions to the world's problems will come from all of us, working at all levels: in our society, in our organizations, and in our own lives. Our publications and resources offer pathways to creating a more just, equitable, and sustainable society. They help people make their organizations more humane, democratic, diverse, and effective (and we don't think there's any contradiction there). And they guide people in creating positive change in their own lives and aligning their personal practices with their aspirations for a better world.

And we strive to practice what we preach through what we call "The BK Way." At the core of this approach is *stewardship,* a deep sense of responsibility to administer the company for the benefit of all of our stakeholder groups, including authors, customers, employees, investors, service providers, sales partners, and the communities and environment around us. Everything we do is built around stewardship and our other core values of *quality, partnership, inclusion,* and *sustainability.*

This is why Berrett-Koehler is the first book publishing company to be both a B Corporation (a rigorous certification) and a benefit corporation (a for-profit legal status), which together require us to adhere to the highest standards for corporate, social, and environmental performance. And it is why we have instituted many pioneering practices (which you can learn about at www.bkconnection.com), including the Berrett-Koehler Constitution, the Bill of Rights and Responsibilities for BK Authors, and our unique Author Days.

We are grateful to our readers, authors, and other friends who are supporting our mission. We ask you to share with us examples of how BK publications and resources are making a difference in your lives, organizations, and communities at www.bkconnection.com/impact.

Dear reader,

Thank you for picking up this book and welcome to the worldwide BK community! You're joining a special group of people who have come together to create positive change in their lives, organizations, and communities.

What's BK all about?

Our mission is to connect people and ideas to create a world that works for all.

Why? Our communities, organizations, and lives get bogged down by old paradigms of self-interest, exclusion, hierarchy, and privilege. But we believe that can change. That's why we seek the leading experts on these challenges—and share their actionable ideas with you.

A welcome gift

To help you get started, we'd like to offer you a **free copy** of one of our bestselling ebooks:

www.bkconnection.com/welcome

When you claim your **free ebook**, you'll also be subscribed to our blog.

Our freshest insights

Access the best new tools and ideas for leaders at all levels on our blog at ideas.bkconnection.com.

Sincerely,

Your friends at Berrett-Koehler

Certified

Corporation